Jimmy!
You have been an inspiration to me in my life. Thank you for the depth of heart in all you

Phil 4:12-13

Wise as Serpents Gentle as Doves

Insight, ideas, and discussion about how to start or improve a church security team

- Purpose/Scope/Goals
- Team Building
- SOGs
- Training
- Communications
- Actions
- More

By: Phil Pinkus
Contributor: David Nixon - EMS SOGs

Copyright © 2018 by Phil Pinkus

All rights reserved. No part of this publication may be reproduced, distributed, or transmitted in any form or by any means, including photocopying, recording, or other electronic or mechanical methods, without the prior written permission of the writer or publisher, except in the case of brief quotations embodied in critical reviews and certain other noncommercial uses permitted by copyright law.

The information in this publication is intended to help ministry leaders better understand general security issues and to aid in the development and management of a worship security team.

No portion of this publication should be used without prior legal review, revision, and approval by an attorney licensed to practice law in your state, and with the full knowledge of your church's insurance company. Author assumes no liability for reliance upon the information provided in this publication.

ISBN-13: 978-1548349691
ISBN-10: 1548349690

All the glory to God! And praise for His direction, instruction, and guidance.

Thanks to my wife Katherina for encouraging and understanding me, for standing by my side as God moved us closer to Him, for allowing me to serve in the capacity I do. I love you and am blessed to have you in my life.

Thank you to Dylan, Magda & Jared, Ally, and Mia. My sacrifices were sometimes only made possible by your yielding's.

To our volunteer security team: Thank you for your heart, your commitment to praise God with excellence, and for your unselfish service. It is my honor to serve with dedicated shepherds. As we pressed for excellence, you did not let politics get in the way

Thank you to entire Salvaggio family for helping me find salvation through Christ Jesus. It only took 14 years, but they never quit.

Many have impacted my life greatly; family, friends, teachers, pastors, etc., but I am including one more person who was a mentor of mine and many others: **Chief Ray Downey – FDNY Special Ops.**

Chief Downey embraced the concept of "Best Practices" for his community, his team members, and the City of New York.

He died on September 11, 2001 in the Twin Towers attack.

Wise as Serpents – Gentle as Doves

Insight, ideas, and discussion about how to start or improve a church security team

Table of Contents

Preface	ix
Forward	xi
Chapter 1: What is Security – "Inside the walls"	1
Chapter 2: Purpose/Scope/Goals & Touch	13
Chapter 3: Developing the team	39
Chapter 4: Training	65
Chapter 5: Protocol	85
Chapter 6: Position Assignments	107
Chapter 7: Chain of Command	113
Chapter 8: Communications	123
Chapter 9: Actions	133
Chapter 10: Firearms	157
Chapter 11: Evacuation/Lockdown	163
Chapter 12: Team Leadership	173
Chapter 13: Conclusion – Then it happened…	181
Appendix	
A. SOG Template	187
B. Worship Security Incident Report	213
C. Threat Checklist	215
D. Training Outline	217
E. Volunteer Security Team	219
F. Bloodborne Pathogens	221
Bibliography	225
Resources	229

Preface

This book should not exist. I should not feel moved to participate on a team dedicated to church security – of all things. But, here we are.

If your church already has a security team in place and are using standard operating guidelines or standard operating procedures, congratulations, you are among the 1%. Please feel free to offer critiques of this book.

If your church has a security team, but is not using a written operating guideline – congratulations, you are among the 10%. This book may not be new to you, but you may find the references helpful. This is where I began my journey in church security.

If your church doesn't have a recognized security team, don't fret, you're in the 90%. There are many resources available to you.

Church violence is on the rise. What once was considered a holy place is now a soft target. Insurance, legal, security, and settlement costs rise along with liability suits. Greater needs for protecting our children against pedophilia, drugs, violence, and other dangers in our churches exist today that were not evident just a decade ago.

In response, churches are starting to realize that volunteer security teams are as necessary as ushers, greeters, and other ministries.

As I began volunteering on my church's security team, the Holy Spirit reached out and instructed me to keep a journal that I would one day share with others who would see the need for an organized volunteer team. This book is not only about operational procedures, it is about my journey to this point.

Completing the first edit of this book in July of 2016, I was excited and emboldened to move ahead. There was some behind the scenes politics, but all in all I was given a "green light" to create SOGs and develop the volunteer security team.

October 5th, 2016, I was called into a meeting where people higher in the organizational ladder decided it was time to put up the, "red light" and everything came to a halt. Change is not usually easy. When you decide to make changes; specific information, reason, and logic should prevail. Hopefully, I have provided all these and more resources in this book. In the end, change is fast when churches are reacting. Being proactive, addressing potential threats before they happen can be a slower process.

Most important – you are not alone. Every team will go through changes. There are many resources available to you. I pray that you find success in your desire to praise God with excellence and that this book provides a bit of insight for you on your journey.

Forward

Wise as Serpents Gentle as Doves is geared toward churches starting a new, or improving an existing church security team. Of all my research on church security, most programs start out discussing logical reasons why security is a necessity in today's modern world. In today's world I question how anyone could make a case against some type of team ready to help the church, its staff, volunteers, congregation, and guests.

Currently in the US, there are 335,000 churches. Only about 10% have any type of security at all. Only a fraction of those who do have an active security team or who employ security guards have a comprehensive plan to guide those teams or protect the flock.

As Christians, obedient to God, we are told by Jesus to act. "Keep watch over yourselves and all the flock of which the Holy Spirit has made you overseers. Be shepherds of the church of God, which he bought with his own blood." – Acts 20:28

Benefits of more detailed structure provide the foundation of instruction, purpose, scope, and goals of the team. Having a written plan will improve performance, strengthen church goals, and reduce church liability.

Many topics will be covered from team formation and membership requirements to meeting and greeting guests, and provide ideas and resources that anyone can implement.

This book is aimed specifically at volunteer security teams. At my church, we pray to God through His Son Jesus Christ to have His hand over us, to protect us from evil, to secure our church and keep us safe. We have a paid security presence. We pay for at least one uniformed police officer to be on campus during services and some events. And, we have a volunteer team of shepherds who watch over the flock during services. We are a threat assessment team that provides immediate response to any incident until outside agencies arrive.

I am an Honorary Member of a Volunteer Fire Department and have been associated with them for over 25 years. Currently, more than 50% of American cities and towns rely on volunteer firefighters to serve their community.

God exposed me to volunteer teams for a reason. We provided fire, EMS, and rescue services to our City and Town that encompassed a 36 mile square area and served about 25,000 people. Volunteers had to attend classes and become certified on every level. David Salvaggio, mentioned on the dedication page, and I, led a technical rescue team whose expertise was mainly extrication and dive rescue, though many of our team were also certified in other specialties. The point here is about dedicated volunteers with servant's hearts and a commitment to excellence. We'll apply these same principles to volunteer security.

Excellence was the expectation and the culture. But more important, was the shepherds who put in the time and energy, some putting in over two thousand hours a year (full time job) as volunteers who sought to serve their community. Do not fear raising standards, it could attract team members who appreciate structure.

The first and primary goal of this book is "how-to" organize, train, and maintain a volunteer security team.

Carl Chinn is an expert in church security. He is the Author of "Evil Invades Sanctuary – The Case for Security in Faith-Based Organizations." But even more important, he is a tremendous resource with a servant's heart. I read his book (Evil Invades Church) and looked up his website, which prompted visitors to seek additional information. Mr. Chinn sent out a couple of emails to church security leaders in my area who invited me to their monthly meeting of church security directors, where information was shared openly among at least two dozen churches that were participating and seeking to provide the best possible volunteer security service to their church.

I had the opportunity to meet Carl at the 2016 National Church Safety & Security Conference held at Rock Church in San Diego, CA - where he was a main speaker. I would like to recap his opening remarks:

In 1963, four young girls were murdered when Klu Klux Clan members placed over a dozen sticks of dynamite underneath a stairway at an entrance of their church - the 16th Street Baptist Church in Birmingham, Alabama. He showed a slide that was divided into four quadrants, each with a picture of the victims and their names. This was the first mass murder in an American church since our founding in 1776 - 187 years. So, we can go back to zero, a time when the thought of a church security team would have been laughable. Carl points out how much the escalation of church violence has risen since then and does a great job of updating his website with major security events at US churches. He has also started the Faith Based Security Network, FBSN (see resources).

Carl Chinn has been involved with a couple of major church incidents himself – the type of incidents that push church elders to create security teams; the type of events we should be prepared for and pray never happen in our community. What stood out to me though was this: American media is based on sensationalism and they readily report the most tragic of stories. We've seen cable news cover horrific events for many days, even weeks after the tragedy is over. But what isn't typically reported, or at least is mentioned for a day and then forgotten, is the violence that occurs when there is no murder involved. I can't tell you if church violence is on the rise or if churches are starting to report it more now than they did in the past; but I can tell you that some church members have taken it upon themselves to become shepherds of their flock. They volunteer or assume the role of "security" and most have no clear direction and could pose huge liability risk to the church they want to protect.

Personally, my feeling is that almost every church already has security of some type; an unofficial person who assumes the role of "protector," you know…the guy who stands at the door and pretends to put his arm around someone as he gives them a quick pat down, checking for weapons; the couple of people gathered together with their conceal carry permits standing ready to protect their church from threats; actual working security teams who work on sheer passion and commitment; or maybe they just have a few cameras and an alarm system. No matter what, I'd be willing to bet that most churches already have some sort of security in place.

I met a person who said he was the only person doing any security at his church. He felt the need and the calling to serve as a volunteer security person. The church had two way radios, but no team, so maybe there was a security team there at one time or maybe the radios were used by technicians. He said he would wear a radio and the earpiece, even though there was no one else to talk to, just to give the impression he was not alone.

While attending the National Church Safety & Security Conference, hosted annually by the San Diego Rock Church, in San Diego, CA, a person stood up on day one and asked how he could create an effective training for a new team. Their church was obviously taking the security ministry very seriously as they sent three of their volunteer security team members and they were looking for answers, as all of us are.

During the next break at the conference, two security team members from another church approached the guy seeking training ideas and were excited to exchange information and share ideas. They said they had an amazing training program, but when asked what it was based upon, they said it was just training scenarios where someone would suggest something and they would play it out. They had no operating procedures that everyone would follow, there was nothing written for the "new guy," on the team and no way to measure their success or evaluate failure.

An executive pastor, from my church, was very concerned about the ability of the church to continue a volunteer security team after current members filtered out, for whatever reason. This is an extremely valid concern and one that caused me to look deeper into how our team was being set up. What I had found was detailed standard operating principles combined with leadership development, created a culture that will exceed me and current team members.

Goal #2: Assure the future of the volunteer security team.

We need to have an honest frank discussion about security teams, their purpose, scope, goals, function, and God's word in relation to this.

In his book, "Serving by Safeguarding Your Church, by Robert H. Welch, he includes a letter in the foreword by Jeff R. Laster who was the first person to greet the stranger walking through the front door of his church. He describes an active shooter incident that happened in his church on September 19, 1999. He succinctly captures the essence of the moment, describing what he saw, heard, and felt. It may have taken me longer to read the foreword than the actual incident which eventually left eight people dead and seven people wounded, as I hung on his every word, I tried to imagine how any team would respond to such chaos.

One line in Jeff's letter hit home. It's a question he was asked while recovering from two gunshot wounds. Sitting in his hospital bed, Jeff asked himself, "What do you think you could have done differently?" It's a question many of us ask and the answer lies in being prepared.

Every church has opportunities to improve whatever security is currently in place. Even though most teams I have met or worked with are volunteer groups, there needs to be a set of guidelines that assure individuals are using "Best Practices" based on the churches goals, which should be rooted in a risk assessment. Risk must include all vulnerabilities, including team safety.

Since I'm asking you to complete an "honest" risk assessment, it's only fair that I share my "honest" assessment of my church. I do this for two reasons: One is, we have now created a system where security "opportunities" are addressed through a chain-of-command, specific people are identified as having responsibility, and the team is committed toward "excellence" in service to God and His church.

It may help for you to know where we started, which is where many will or have started, and how we fashioned our team to meet church goals and protect risks exposed in a risk assessment.

"Frustration" is the result of prevention of the progress, success, or fulfillment of something. I have felt a lot of frustration and obstruction in a church where people appreciate our efforts and support our purpose. My prayers include asking for direction, instruction, and guidance (D.I.G.) (Thank you to James Morrisey Director of D.I.G. IT Ministries). It is what has kept my head aimed in the right direction. All the glory to God and following His path, our team has greatly expanded and improved. But, truth be told, it has not been as easy as I would have anticipated.

When I joined the volunteer security team, there were no Standard Operating Guides (SOGs) or Standard Operating Procedures (SOPs), which is actually very common when it comes to church security teams. Guidelines outlining how, when, or where a security was to respond was left up the individual responder. There was no written plan that could be easily followed or taught to new team members.

Questions require answers, but the chain of command also needed definition. Issues went unanswered, though early discussions with other team members quickly revealed that some type of structure would have been appreciated.

Regularly scheduled training was not performed and response to security breaches was unorganized. There was a huge opportunity to increase operational effectiveness, build a team, expand services, and focus on excellence. Most important, we could employ safety precautions to protect team members, pastors, staff, volunteers, and church members. But also important is reducing liability exposures to the church and individual security team members.

Please know that I have only respect and gratitude for everyone who serves with the passion of Jesus Christ in their heart. Being able to critique a system prior to a major incident is a gift and an opportunity to be thankful for. We pray before we serve and always ask God to protect us and keep the church safe. But, sometimes our abilities and faith is tried and it is our responsibility to navigate that test in the direction the Lord expects. Even King David, who enjoyed the hand of God in defeating his enemies, was instructed to build walls and protect them. God was directly involved in the victories of David's armies, as God used the "armies of men" to defeat threats to King David and the Jews. A purposeful volunteer security team fills this element of God's protection for us.

As the "new guy" at a big church, I didn't know many people at all. When I started, ushers and others who were not on the security team began identifying themselves to me, telling me they have my back and that they were carrying concealed firearms. Arizona is a conceal carry state with no license required. Short of posting a "No Firearms" sign on the doors, there was not much we could do to prevent anyone from bringing firearms into the church. Again, guidelines needed to be developed to give the church more control.

On my first Sunday on the team, I was taken on a tour of the campus and discussed operations with the head of security. He said I should look for people acting weird and be wary of anyone carrying a backpack. He covered radio communications and described the different security teams. Yet, no other security team member was checking bags or communicating that they saw people who peaked their interest or who looked like they just didn't belong. I had no idea what my authority was, which was really a moot point, because no one else knew who I was either. We had no uniforms, identifying badges, etc. Most people weren't even aware that a security team existed.

In the second of two Sunday services, I was given different directions by no less than four people. One was a security team member, one was a pastor, and two were ushers. None of these people were the team leader or the head of security. As I tried to figure out who was in charge, I found frustration in the fact that no one could give me an answer. Understandably, at a larger church there can be more confusion, but the overall message is about having procedures in place.

Our church has a main floor that holds about thirty-five hundred people and two levels of mezzanine seating, each with a capacity of about one thousand. At any given service, there could be as many as three thousand people on average – Christmas, Easter and special events tend to attract larger crowds. Imagine my attempt to comprehend the situation as one person says go to the third floor, another says stand by the main door on the first floor, and…well…you get the point. And if I'm confused, you can bet any new security team member would be also.

There are at least five layers of active security at my church. One person was in charge of hiring uniformed security guards who were present day and night, three hundred and sixty five days a year. These people were charged with watching the entire campus, which included two worship buildings, a school, children's center, gymnasium, an administration building, and I believe we also had our own Starbucks on campus. There were also several large parking lots on about 72 acres of land that abutted a mountain. Uniformed paid security guards were hired to deter crime on the campus, identify suspicious activity, and make the right reports. They were not very apparent during church services and basically avoided the main sanctuary unless they were called in to help.

Another layer of security was our outside volunteer security and transportation. Cart drivers were responsible for transporting visitors from the parking lot to the church's main entrance. After services started, carts were plugged into electrical outlets to recharge the batteries. Outside security and transporters took a break until services ended. They operated on a different radio channel than our inside security team. I couldn't get a clear picture of the effectiveness of two security teams operating on two different channels or why the teams were separate, and there was basically little to no outside coverage during services.

The third layer of our volunteer security team inside the sanctuary during church services. Again, we were using a different radio channel than other security team. Our charge was to protect the pastor, the congregation, and church property – including offerings – during the church services, which were held on Wednesday night, Saturday night, and twice on Sunday morning.

A fourth level of security is the personal protection detail provided to senior pastors.

Assuring the future of the volunteer security team requires a structure and a process that new leaders can utilize to make decisions and train new recruits. This allows the team to set goals together and work towards achievement. Long term shared goals bond teams and creates longevity.

Goal #3 is coordination of efforts.

Our fifth level of security includes at least one off duty uniformed police officer assigned to the church during worship services. He typically was stationed at the usher station in the lobby area of the building through the offering and was then free to roam inside or outside of the building and direct traffic before and after services. He too had a church radio, but was always tuned into the outside security team, because those were his instructions. The officer was also our go-to-guy for extra help, including emergency medical services (EMS) calls when needed. But, to get to him, we had to turn our radios to a different channel, which in the heat of the moment can cost precious time and without procedures can be very confusing.

According to statistics, 53% of major church incidents happen outside of the church and 47% happen inside. We'll go over our security practices of Deter, Detect, Delay, and Deny throughout this book.

One big question needed to be resolved is: In any incident big enough to warrant calling in outside services, who is in charge before they arrive? Who will command the incident until outside agencies arrive? Determining "Who" will take charge in a bigger incident is important. Teams need a leader who is able to lead and who has a vision and a plan. Team leaders need to know if they are leading or if someone else is giving directions and it needs to be decided before an incident happens. This will be discussed more, later in the book, where post incident planning will also be discussed.

After a short while, I began talking with others on the security team. Some had been on the team for many years. I asked about processes, like who is responsible for calling 911 in an emergency? What are the evacuation procedures? Who is in charge of making sure the automatic defibrillator's batteries are charged or replaced and much more. I got a lot of, "I think," and "Well, that's a good question." So I was not the only person in the dark and this was by no means unique to my church – it just so happened to be where I was.

What I have learned is that holes or gaps create opportunities to fill the voids. I believe that every organization, business, school, service provider, etc. has a responsibility to its members, customers, or attendees to critique current operations honestly, identify opportunities to make improvements, create plans to achieve those goals, implement the changes, hold ongoing training of the new processes and/or procedures, and then assure changes are made according to the plan.

Our goal is to help make those systems more efficient, increase safety, reduce liability, make congregants feel more secure, help those who seek to find the Lord, and hopefully allow church attendees to feel safer in the worship environment. I have found outside organizations ranging from the FBI to the Department of Homeland Security and local police and fire. There are Associations and churches dedicated specifically to the operations, training, etc., of volunteer church security teams. And there are professional associations such as the Association of Threat Assessment Professionals (ATAP), ASIS International, Christian Emergency Network (CEN) and others who provide very detailed information about formation and operations of soft target security teams.

Church security is a growing trend in response to people who have access to the church, its congregation, contents, etc. Though the crazed active killer is a top concern on the long list of concerns, it is not typically the activity most church security teams respond to and it should not be the sole purpose of a security team.

People who disrupt church usually fall into a few categories: threats from people under stress (angry), threats from individuals with altered states of consciousness, political objectors, etc. We invite the "broken" into worship with the hope that they will find salvation through Jesus Christ.

Security teams prepared to "Deter" those thinking of disrupting, "Detecting" people who are not deterred, "Delaying" those who are not detected, and "denying" active safety threats must be trained according to operating guides that take them through processes step-by-step.

Matthew 10:16 - "Behold, I send you out as sheep in the midst of wolves; so be wise as serpents and innocent as doves."

Goal #4: Provide an SOG template that you can alter to fit your church's volunteer security needs.

This book started as a personal journal, as our church's team was/is being reorganized. I'm the new guy, but I have a background in security that includes crowd control, personal security protection, maintaining security posts and I served as a firefighter/EMT in my community for almost two decades. Rescue certifications include: vehicle and heavy machinery extrication, dive team, confined space rescue, hazardous materials through level A, and a long list that also includes FEMA terrorist response and building collapse. I taught these skills to hundreds of fire firefighters over the years, through a nonprofit group Code III, through my fire department, and through several commercial businesses. I've seen a lot of destruction, pain, and confusion and have always have felt blessed to be the person running into a situation everyone else is running out of. Though

I've trained a lot, I continue to learn. This will never end.

Understandably, in every church there are personal political implications, turf wars, job protectionism, and misunderstanding. I continue to find a few walls even though we are well past the restructuring process, though generally we are way ahead of where we were when I started.

I am thankful for our church pastors and security leaders who supported changes and helped me navigate the politics. But no transition is ever that smooth, especially when the changes are not modest. I'm trying to avoid using the term drastic, because any change for some people is drastic. However, everyone's input and ideas continue to be very helpful and I appreciate the guidance.

Since our focus is improving the team efforts and response, and because we are, at the initial writing of this book – going through the process ourselves, I thought it would be a great opportunity to document and discuss our team's growth, challenges', failures, and successes.

Along with our main church, two satellite churches have joined our group and it was the intention that all campuses will be trained using one SOG template. You have permission to use these templates freely. They were written to be duplicable at any church. Feel free to copy any and all parts for your team.

Sustaining any team must include recruiting, organizing, communications, and leadership development. All are topics of discussion in this book. Churches must also be prepared to handle post incident operations. Worst case scenarios can include unknown people showing up, describing themselves as "experts," and flooding your church with recovery assistance. Weeks of news coverage could damage a church reputation and cost membership, tithing, and contributions. Protests could erupt. And annual memorials could continually stir memories.

Securing a church goes well beyond a person standing at the door. Today's world is much different than the world I was raised in. Desires to protect our church against those who would disrupt us, or to offer the best possible outcome to God's children, is to use best practices to start, grow, and organize a volunteer security team.

Chapter 1

WHAT IS SECURITY – "INSIDE THE WALLS"

Before we can go further, we need take a glimpse at what security means. What does security look like?

Biblical

1 Peter 5:2 (NIV) – "Be shepherds of God's flock that is among you, watching over it, not because you must but because you want to, and not greedily but eagerly, as God desires." Then in 1 Peter 5:8, we are instructed, "Be clear-minded and alert. Your opponent, the Devil, is prowling around like a roaring lion, looking for someone to devour."

The Bible has many mentions of being alert, watchful, and aware. "Watch for enemies." "Be alert for error." "Be aware of your own condition." "Look at what you are doing." "Know where you are." Ephesians 6:18 – "be alert with your most diligent efforts;" 1 Peter 1:13 – "Therefore, prepare your minds for action, keep a clear head, and set your hope completely on the grace to be given you when Jesus, the Messiah, is revealed;" 1 Thessalonians 5:6 – "Therefore, let's not fall asleep like others do, but let's stay awake and be sober;" Matthew 24:43 – "But be sure of this: if the owner of the house had known when during the night the thief would be coming, he would have stayed awake and not allowed his house to be broken into." And thus, we are instructed to always be aware.

In the "Sermon on the Mount," Jesus instructs us: Matthew 5:43 – 48 (NIV) – "Love for Enemies." 43 "You have heard that it was said, 'Love your neighbor and hate your enemy.' 44 But I tell you, love your enemies and pray for those who persecute you, 45 that you may be children of your Father in heaven. He causes his sun to rise on the evil and the good, and sends rain on the righteous and the unrighteous. 46 If you love those who love you, what reward will you get? Are not even the tax collectors doing that? 47 And if you greet only your own people, what are you doing more than others? Do not even pagans do that? 48 Be perfect, therefore, as your heavenly Father is perfect."

This must be the foundation of every church security team. While there is great value in finding people with current and/or prior law enforcement or military backgrounds, we need to be sure that even they have this heart for this ministry. Security does not have to be threatening, uniformed, or heavy handed. Your security team should add to the importance of greeters and ushers. They should be able to be alert for potential disrupters and have the ability to try and calm disruptions with a Jesus-like heart. And yet, they need to be able to take appropriate action when necessary.

Psalms 122:7 – 7 (NIV) God says to King David, "Peace be within thy walls, and prosperity within thy palaces." Peace inside the walls is achieved with trained armies who respond to threats. I believe this also applies to church security teams. Psalms 46-48 offer praise to God and recognize that it is His will that defeats enemies and armies. Yet, the people contemplate Zion's defense, viewed from the perspective of what they have "seen" at the temple," and refer to the strength of Zion's "towers," "ramparts" and "citadels," and they take on an active role in their defense, knowing that it is God that gives them the power to overcome those who would attempt to do them harm. God does not eliminate their enemies or "Keep peace," on His own – in this case – even though He certainly does have that power.

Just to complete the picture, a "citadel" is a fortress, typically on high ground, protecting or dominating a city." Interesting that David writes about the awesome power of God to defeat enemies, and yet has dominant forces in place to protect the city. Their awesome structure serves as a deterrent to those who would consider threatening the peace within the walls. We know the power of God to include His ability to smite the earth if it is His will.

The people of Zion did not simply stand on the wall and wait for something to happen, they were aware. They stood watch and actively trained to detect potential threats. They trained to respond, to delay or de-escalate threats inside the walls. And, when threats went undeterred, undetected, and could not be de-escalated, David's armies were blessed with the hand of God to overcome their enemies.

Pastor Greg Laurie spoke at our church recently and said, "God uses people to achieve his will." When you think about it, tithes and offerings are not collected unless someone volunteers to pass and collect the bucket. The same is true of a volunteer security team. We seek men and women who have a desire to serve with compassion, but who are also brave enough to stand up to the evil that gets inside our walls. We are looking for shepherds to tend the flock.

Threats and Violence – "Inside our walls"

Regardless of how we interpret our guidance on the issue of church violence or how we are going to prepare our congregation to deal with it when evil gets inside our "walls," the rising rage and violence in the world is undeniable.

Statistics and stories will be shared throughout this book. Yes, we do consider active shooter(s) in all of our plans, as it is the pinnacle of any disruption – no matter how small it seems when it starts. But that is a worst case scenario, a training goal under which all other incidents will be addressed properly when risk assessed correctly and addressed according to written response policies.

There are many other "threats" that we respond to and should be concerned about. Our team is officially referred to as "Threat assessment and Immediate Response team. We are responsible for security from the time before an incident happens, until it's over, or until local outside agencies arrive and relieve us from their incident command chain.

Prison populations are swollen with pedophiles, drug abusers, violent criminals, thieves, gang members, murderers, etc. Our courts are clogged and backlogged with cases yet to be heard and sometimes these people are free on bail or remanded to house arrest, or even let go on their own recognizance to roam the streets. Certainly there are times when a person in crisis finds themselves at a church and accepts salvation through Jesus Christ; however, there are also times when people in crisis find opportunities to disrupt or threaten soft targets.

Criminal background checks may only expose the crime a person trying to get into our good graces has committed. A person could have been arrested for something major, charged with something lower, and pleaded guilty to something even much less. Bottom line is, bad people will try to get into our walls by acting like good people, and their available history doesn't always present all the facts.

Alleviating their huge court load, District Attorneys, public defenders, and judges rely heavily on plea bargaining that reduce criminal complaints, reduce sentences, and can even offer nothing more than a slap on the wrists. Calling a criminal a "First offender," is a misnomer. They are most likely not "first offenders," they are merely caught for the first time.

Pedophiles have a strong, almost irresistible, desire to have sex with children. The average pedophile molests 260 victims during their lifetime. According to Ernie Allen, President of the National Center for Missing and Exploited Children, "There are 400,000 registered sex offenders in the United States, and an estimated 80 to 100,000 of them are missing. They're supposed to be registered, but we don't know where they are and we don't know where they're living."

When a potential volunteer goes through a background check, all we find is what they were charged with. A thief pleads guilty to trespassing and the state reduces the charges of burglary. We may never know they were thieves and we allow them into our walls.

Media blasts news that negatively affects the church. So, we constantly hear about most heinous crimes, the murders, the child sex, the pastor caught with a prostitute, etc. If only they covered the news of every person that was saved by God's mercy and grace…but they don't. What is missing is all the crime, violence and threats that churches have to deal with in today's world – and the numbers are staggering.

Church violence is not always about intruders. Often, it comes from our own congregation. Anger is our enemy.

From his Series: The Guidelines Commentary, FEBRUARY 3, 2015 (ENGLISH), Dr. Harold J. Sala writes, "It is no wonder that Paul advised, "If it is possible, as far as it depends on you, live at peace with everyone" (Romans 12:18). True, there is a disclaimer that you find in that conditional phrase, "if it is possible." There are times when peace is not a possibility…"

Anger can trigger outbursts inside our walls. The anger doesn't have to be aimed at ministry; it can be between married people, friends, business associates, volunteers, youth, etc. Outbursts of anger must be diffused quickly. Yet, there may come a time when the ministry, ushers, and even security teams cannot de-escalate the situation and the angry person becomes a greater threat.

You could probably add a lot to this list. Violent video games, movies, and music that promotes the thug life, drugs and alcohol, gang protectionism, absent parents, sexually abused children who become sex abusers, and so much more that people have to deal with all compile this list. All are reasons why churches should have a trained security team to protect them inside their walls.

Breaking down security considerations/needs – "Inside our walls"

Throughout this book we will be discussing "Risk Assessment." It is a process of trying to identify every aspect of risk exposure, on every level. Risk assessments can be conducted by paid professionals or by volunteers. Since this book is geared toward volunteer security teams, we will look at the option of in-house risk assessments by volunteers who are not professional risk assessment specialists. Also available, the Department of Homeland Security (DHS) does offer risk assessment services. (see resources)

Conducting a risk assessment can be as simple as following a checklist, assessing which concerns can or should be addressed first, and then implementing a plan. Sheepdog Church Security does have a very good risk assessment checklist that "relies heavily on guidelines provided by the American Crime Prevention Institute and the discontinued website Church Safety (dot) com. Sheepdog Church Security has downloadable training bundles that I have used as a trusted resource. In all fairness, I will disclose that I am a dues paying member of Sheepdog Church Security and that I have paid for training materials from them. They are one of many resources we will discuss. Pastor Jimmy Meeks is an amazing trainer.

Included in the risk assessment are the following groups of concerns that rely on honest assessment by church leaders: Neighborhood, the perimeter of the church – including church grounds and the building perimeter, alarm systems, access control, video cameras, the inside of the building, managing who has access to keys, property inventories, youth security, financial security, assessing the volunteer security team, EMS response, violence response, firearm considerations, and other considerations. The assessment guides users to look at their situation and helps prompt solutions.

Our team works on the premise of understand the risk, address the risk, and act/respond quickly. We have to understand/identify our risks to be able to address them. This enables us to create a plan that allows us to respond quicker.

Church Security needs

I was baptized at smaller Inner City Baptist church by Pastor Joe Dallas. According to an article on the Pastoral Care, Inc., website (http://www.pastoralcareinc.com/articles/bi-vocational-pastors/) "The Baptist organization is the leader in promoting and supporting bi-vocational pastors. They report that 75% of their churches run under 100 people, many of which are bi-vocational. The Nazarene Church reports that about 40% of their ministers are bi-vocational. The Pentecostal churches also report a number of their pastors working outside of the ministry due to declining attendance. While George Barna reports that 87% of Protestant churches have full-time ministers." Similar to the church I was baptized in, we see in many cases there is not much of a budget even for paying the pastor.

Throughout this book, we will explore cost saving opportunities. In the chapter where we discuss training, I write about my experience training firefighters from other departments. Theses departments ran the spectrum of funding, just as churches do. In our quest for excellence, we cannot compare what others have the ability to pay for, only that they maximize practices of excellence based upon their ability, so please don't look at the following list as daunting or unachievable. Risk assessing will bring to light things that may need immediate attention and will allow for future planning.

Every church is different. The church I serve now has 5 campuses and each one is unique. When you are aware of the full picture, and you complete your individual risk assessment, you can pick and choose what works for your individual church. You can modify practices and policies at any time.

Just as with any other endeavor, security practices, policies, and procedures are constantly changing. It is important to have at least 1 person designated to stay abreast. I have found conferences very informative. They also provide the opportunity for team leaders to share information. Less expensive is membership to church security associations. At the very least, free online subscriptions can be very insightful. Information can also be found for free on the internet.

Service protection

We'll start with security protection during scheduled services as this is when most people are present and risks are higher. At churches where personnel are present during off service hours, full time during the week, we find there is a similar need for security, working the week, though typically this would require a full time or paid security guard.

Our volunteers are trained to detect people who do not fit the flow of normal congregants. Normal flow is referred to as "baseline." When a person is identified as suspicious, we refer to them as people of interest (POI) or "doesn't look right (DLR). This is not a judgment, just an observation. This is our "threat assessment," portion of the job. The meat of this book is about volunteer security teams operations and we will discuss this in much more detail.

Our role is to protect the pastor, protect the staff, volunteers, and congregation – in that order. We achieve our goals through risk assessing and identifying opportunities a threat could expose. Volunteers typically fill this role. The bigger the church gets, the bigger the team may be, and the more ability we have to develop a budget specifically for security.

Campus security outside of services

This refers to the parking lot, play grounds, public gathering places, where people move before or after planned services. Again, volunteers can staff these positions. The goals are to show presence, to deter potential threats from carrying out a disturbance. When volunteers are obvious, and they are plentiful, some people who were contemplating a crime or disruption may rethink it. When nothing happens – we are most successful.

Some churches have golf cart services, parking directors, greeters, and ushers outside. All these people can be trained to be observant and have the ability to get ahold of security to follow up on people of interest.

Goals are to prevent break-ins with buildings and cars. To be able to help a person who may be having a medical emergency, or help with a dead car battery. They can spot liabilities, like oil spills or gas leaks, car lights left on by accident, or kids skateboarding in areas where they shouldn't be.

Special events

These could be a Christian singles group, sisterhood, men's club, teens, athletics, and other events, meetings, or gatherings where more people are in attendance. Again, these are soft targets with fewer people able to defend themselves. As our team grows, we have more people power to cover requests for volunteer security coverage.

June 17th, 2015, the Charleston NC church massacre was a mass shooting, that took place at the Emanuel African Methodist Episcopal Church. During the hour preceding the attack, 13 people including the shooter participated in the Bible study. This was an event separate from church services.

December 9, 2007, a 24-year-old male opened fire at the Youth with a Mission (YAM) training center in Arvada, Colorado with a pistol, killing two and wounding two others before escaping. YAM was holding a Christmas banquet that had taken place earlier that night. This was also a special event.

Your team may have the ability to establish presence. Most likely, the response won't be for an active killer – the new term to describe more than just a shooter. A couple weeks ago a teen girl hit another young woman and gave her a bloody nose at a teen event on our campus. It was the mother of the girl who got hit that ended up becoming the uncontrollable person in the room. Again, you will constantly see worst case scenarios in books, training, and discussions about church security. But, it's the everyday happenings that don't make the news or crime reports that a trained security team can help with.

Personal Protection

Personal protection (PP) is usually afforded to senior pastors at our church. It's not just the words they share, but they are the visionaries, the ones who set the pace and the goals. Additionally, they are the ones capable of raising the funds that make everything work. Losing a key person over a small or large incident could be a key to losing church membership, volunteers, and even staff. For this reason, we assign specific people as "personal protection."

Personal protection for pastors would require another book. We'll discuss it a little, but the National Organization of Church Security and

Safety Management (NOCSSSM) (www.nocssm.org) had some good information on this. Personal protection could include details on mission trips, out of area travel, including foreign countries, and in some cases may require 24/7 protection. Personal protection may be volunteer, or a combination of both.

Securing our children

Youth risks can be found in the church, schools, camps & conference centers, child services, after school programs, teen socials, youth sports, day cares, preschools, child services, and more. The first step is training staff and volunteers to be aware of child sexual abuse signs and to recognize suspicious activity of others. Volunteers should be screened and put through a background check. And, there should be oversight by the church. They should be strongly encouraged to report any signs of child sexual predator activities.

While this is a huge concern to everyone involved, discussion in this book is pretty much limited to background checks. Ministry Safe, (www.ministrysafe.com) is one of the best resources I have found for church training on child sexual predator awareness. They have an excellent 5 point training program and certification. They can also assist with child ID programs and suggest policies and procedures.

Physical security

Physical Security is another aspect of securing our churches. It deals with structures and physical layouts/designs, and encompasses things like lighting, fencing, cameras, alarms, doors, windows, and physical barriers. Again, this is an area that the security director should be at least a little familiar with. An Association called ASIS (www.asisonline.org) offers Physical Security Professional (PSP)® certification for "demonstrated experience in physical security assessment, the application, design and integration of physical security systems, and implementation of physical security measures."

It's not that we all have to be Physical Security certified, but we should at least be knowledgeable enough to discuss it and understand the principles. I've seen church security teams that don't have plans and deter intruders and avert potential threats – including some that could result in liability suits against the church.

A person familiar with physical security should be included in new construction and remodeling plans. Costs to implement physical security barriers can be more efficient if applies during the construction stage.

Recently, one terrorist tactic that has become pretty popular is killing and maiming people with vehicles. We've seen a lot on the news about the use of bigger trucks, especially in Europe, but here in America there have been vehicular assaults using cars and pickup trucks.

As our church added a new addition, physical barriers on sidewalks were not really a consideration. Now they are. Having the foresight to install these barriers during construction may have reduced costs.

IT Security

Certainly this is not a topic I will be writing much about, however, it should be a huge concern to any church with a membership list. ASIS and the FBI Infraguard program are great sources of information. Infraguard and ASIS both have cyber information centers that church IT people can access information from. "Infraguard," (www.infraguard.org) is a partnership between the FBI and members of the private sector. The InfraGard program provides a vehicle for seamless public-private collaboration with government that expedites the timely exchange of information and promotes mutual learning opportunities relevant to the protection of Critical Infrastructure." You must pass an FBI background check to join, but the information has been amazing and membership is free. Infraguard also updates on terrorist threats and terror activities in the US and abroad.

More

A few other areas security should be concerned with are protecting the churches name, reducing liability claims, of course active shooter, and I do discuss that in more detail. But there is whole other area of planning for post active shooter events.

"Post active shooter" begins when the shooting starts. The flow of response to an active shooter is run, hide, fight. In a recent ASIS webcast on post active shooter planning, Steven Crimando MA, CTS, CHA-V used the following words to describe the post incident process: "Stop the killing, stop the bleeding, and stop the crying."

Regardless or your church size, location, teachings, fund raising ability, etc, recognize that violence in America is increasing. We have a responsibility to provide a level of security that is the best we can offer with the resources we have. We are charged in Psalm 82:4 to "Rescue the weak and the needy; deliver them from the hand of the wicked."

Today's security requirements are vastly more complex than they were even a few years ago. Understand what you can provide and use resources to find information to start or improve your team's level of protection. 2 Peter 1:3 "His divine power has given us everything we need for life and godliness through the full knowledge of the one who called us by his own glory and excellence." He has given us shepherds who want to help protect the flock. Use them to start or grow a volunteer security team at your church. Support them and their mission. Give them direction, instruction, and guidance – which is what the rest of this book is about.

Chapter 2

PURPOSE/SCOPE/GOALS & TOUCH

Firefighting/EMS and technical rescue provided me a great opportunity to help others. It allowed me to give to my community using my time and talents, which are God's gifts. Continually pushing myself and my team to learn more, we took the initiative to raise response capabilities, increase safety to rescuers, and build a sustainable program in the community. Thankful for opportunity to serve others, we felt responsible to be the best that we could be. Excellence was the goal. Someone on our team was always training somewhere and they brought their knowledge back to the firehouse and shared with those who wanted to be the best.

Our responsibility as leaders, officers, first responders, and members of the community meant protecting everyone involved. This included firefighters, EMS, police, other responders and their families to make sure we were using the latest and greatest tactics that included improving safety of the team. Mike Diggs, Safety Director for Rock Church in San Diego summed it up best when he asked, "Do we want a win, or do we want excellence?"

Interestingly, assembling a group of volunteer firefighters that want it all – dive rescue, extrication, farm rescue, high angle, hazardous materials, confined space rescue, was not an easy task. Higher officers and longtime department members were concerned that we were trying to "split" the department. They didn't see the need or believed we could achieve as much as we did. We ran into opposition from firefighters who sided with officers. Yet, we continually recruited, forged ahead, and in time, due to national standards changing, liability issues, and increased awareness of the need for higher trained people, fire department leadership eventually came around.

In writing these SOGs I have been challenged by both my church and our Director of Security who I initially reported to. Yet, all the glory to God, but we push on, recruit new members, drive the team forward, raise up leaders, and continue to learn new processes and procedures that we can take back and train others to do.

I was also blessed to work with Ron Naab, who at the time was Deputy Chief of the Allenton Fire Department, and his nonprofit group, Code III in WI. Ron is a warrior for Christ with an amazing depth of care and concern for his fellow man. We taught car, bus, and semi-truck extrication, farm rescue, confined space and other technical rescue classes to hundreds and hundreds of firefighters from several states.

Departments that participated on our training opportunities varied in size, including all types of budgets, membership, community size, response area, etc. They were large, tiny, and everything in between. They had different gear, tools, trucks, processes. Desiring to be the best or committing to "excellence," can sometimes seem expensive and too distant to visualize – especially with volunteers.

I was blessed to come from a fire department whose community created a foundation for fundraising that exceeded many other departments' wildest dreams. It would be easy to look at a smaller program and criticize, but the hearts and commitment from my brothers and sisters at these departments was equal to, if not greater than, many team members on my department. There cannot be any judgment regarding limitations when it comes to budget, only that departments should accept the responsibility to be the best they can be with the resources available.

Purpose/Scope/Goals & Touch | 15

This goes for churches as well.

It is the goal of this book to be that resource to help your church staff, ministries, congregants, and volunteers realize the safest, most fulfilling experiences that invite others to find the forgiveness, mercy, and grace that provides the greatest peace and healing. There have been many occasions when church pastors, staff, and volunteers have been alarmed at someone who entered the building that just didn't fit in or look right. They were very relieved to have a team dedicated to meet these concerns.

The SOGs provided in this book are free. Training can be free. Other things may be available at minimal costs. But the bottom line is that money should not be an obstacle to providing the best level of security your church is capable of. As you go through these SOGs be sure and include your church's insurance company and attorney. Utilize free resources like the Department of Homeland Security, FBI, FEMA, local police and fire, and other resource or sharing opportunities listed in this book.

I have met a lot of security directors and team members who love what they do and appreciate the opportunity to reach out to others. Always remember these resources are available to you as well.

The first step is determining a shared purpose for the security team. We use the term, "Volunteer Security Team," though that wasn't always the case. When I started with the team, we were, "Inside Security." Later, when the first SOGs were developed, we were the, "Worship Service Security Team."

Then, the team voted to become, "Shepherds." This name was to reflect biblical teachings of protectors who are not paid. But higher ups decided that the word "Shepherd," would apply to anyone who steered the flock in the right direction and they decided that our team should not have a corner on that name.

As it came to pass, we decided to call ourselves exactly what we are – "Volunteer Security Team." This allowed us to change our "Purpose" statement and expand our services beyond worship. I actually do like it better, because it defines us more correctly. And yes, there was another change…we recently added EMS, whose SOGs are mixed in with security, but we are now officially: Volunteer Security/EMS team.

Not sure about every state, but in California any group with the name "Security," in it must register team members as guards, license them with the state, and jump though certain hoops, which is why many churches in that state will call themselves "Safety Teams." Make sure the name suits the purpose. It defines exactly what we do – provide security. And so filling in the rest of the blanks is easy.

I've read about many churches, and have firsthand experience with many other church security team members, about the need and perceptions of church security teams. Attend any church security seminar or conference and you will see the same thing. Thus, it is important to draw an accurate picture of the exact purpose of the team so that church leaders who will be discussing, approving, and funding this mission will have a better understanding of exactly what the group will look like and where it wants to go.

Remember, most likely a person or people already in your church are acting as your churches security and are ready to react during services to any threats they perceive. I'm not an attorney, but even though these people and their actions are not organized by the church, you'd better believe that the church will be accountable for their actions. This could include civil liabilities, adverse press and public relations, and loss of congregants.

As I started writing this book, an incident took place in Norristown, PA – "A Lansdale man, identified as 46 year old man has been charged with Voluntary Manslaughter and Reckless Endangerment for the shooting death of a 27 year old fellow church member at Keystone Fellowship Church."

Apparently, the 27 year old was looking for a place to sit down. When he found an empty seat someone tapped him on the shoulder and told him the seat was reserved and an argument ensued. An associate pastor and couple of ushers attended to the disturbance and decided to let 27 year old stay in his seat, successfully deescalating the situation.

Within seconds, the 46 year old approached the younger man with a badge in one hand and a pistol in the other. With the pistol pointed at him, the younger man punched the older one with the gun. The audience of about 300 heard the bang, bang and watched the 27 year old die in his seat at the hands of a man almost twice his age.

The older man was not a police officer. There was no church security team. His badge said, "Concealed Carry Permit Holder." The badge was purchased online by the older guy, who had passed his conceal carry permitting process just two weeks earlier.

Lead Pastor John Cope, in his first sermon after the deadly shooting asks, "Can events define us?" He talks about two families from his church that are forever affected. You see, both men and their families had attended that church for over 7 years. He then talks about the fear fellow parishioners feel.

Earlier I cited a phrase: Stop the killing (that refers to the killing mechanism), Stop the bleeding (treat all patients), and Stop the crying (the traumatic event that will affect everyone). This takes planning and training – and even them mistakes will be made.

Imagine that a homeless person came in to your service to warm up one cold and blistery winter morning. Your first thought is that they need a bath and they appear drunk or stoned as they slur their words. A team member without SOGs or an individual who has assumed the role of "security" or "protector" approaches the homeless person and asks them to leave. He believes he's doing what's in the best interest of the church and says in a kind Christ-like way, "Sir, I'm going to have to ask you to leave."

Turning his head toward the "Shephard," the homeless guy wants to talk, but before he can utter a word the self-appointed church guard smells the fruity scent of alcohol on the drifter's breath. Now convinced that person is drunk, the security person grabs him by the arm to usher him out. Fairly harmless, except that the security guy doesn't know that fruity scent is actually a result of diabetes, a condition called diabetic ketoacidosis.

Not that this is in any way going to be a medical or first response book, but… Diabetic ketoacidosis (DKA) can lead to diabetic coma or even death. When blood cells don't get the glucose they need for energy, the body begins to burn fat for energy, producing ketones. The body does this when it doesn't have enough insulin to use glucose. When ketones build up in the blood, it becomes more acidic and the scent has been described as fruity like nail polish remover. Many responders have assumed this is a result of intoxication, which can produce a similar breath scent.

Once at the main door, the man braces against the cold glass and the security person accidently pushes the diabetic homeless person outside a little too hard. But, because his blood sugars are low, the displaced person slips on the ice and can't regain his balance. He falls and breaks his arm on the concrete steps – or conjure up any odd possibility.

Please do not imagine that your congregant who assumed the security role couldn't possibly be arrested for assault and battery, if the man presses charges. When and if the media gets wind of this, and/or as you are sued in civil court, you learn that the church has no liability insurance coverage for your actions, because a volunteer security team was not included in the policy. An eager lawyer approaches their client, the person who, thanks to you and your insurance company probably won't be homeless any more, and offer their services for free, because no one should be treated in this way, especially in a house of God. Yes, God does work in mysterious ways.

I can see it now…the plaintiff's lawyer has summoned your church leaders to the stand. One by one they ask, "Do you have a formal security team?" And, one by one each leader tells the truth, "No, our church does not have a security team." And you may feel as though you are in the clear, because it is clear to you that the church never condoned a security person, team, or ministry.

But then, the "wooden stake" questions are asked, "Do you know the person who acted like church security?" The honest answer is, "Yes." Then finally, "Did you have any knowledge that this person was acting as a security figure in the church?" And again, you have to answer honestly. And, if you had any knowledge, or even a suspicion, and your leaders allowed this to happen – they condoned it and the church now shares liability, because the reality is, even if just one person is acting like security and you know it – you have a church security team. You chose to have the comfort of safety without having the responsibility of control.

The church must retain more control of their security team (in this instance). A good starting point is in writing out the purpose, scope, and goals of the Volunteer Security Team.

Excerpted from John Baldoni's book, Lead with Purpose: To define the purpose, you want to ask three questions:

"What is our vision? This question is aspirational. What do we want to become? Just as young people ask this question upon choosing a career, organizations need to do the same. Vision emerges from the sense of purpose. It forms the "why," but it also embraces the future as in "to become" the best, the most noted the highest quality, or the most trusted.

What is our mission? Very often this is the easiest to answer because all you need to do is look around at what you are doing. Your mission is the "what" of an organization. For example, if you work in a mental health facility, your mission is to care for and provide therapy to those who suffer from conditions that inhibit their ability to learn, study, work, and get along with others.

What are our values? Neither vision, nor mission mean much if they are not reinforced by strong values. Values shape the culture—that is, the way people behave toward others. Ethics and integrity must be a given. But people want more than good behavior; they want to work in a place where cooperation and collaboration are norms. They want also to know their work matters and they will be recognized for it. Values enforce the behaviors that employees cherish.

Now that you know the questions, what can you do about it? Make time at staff meetings to discuss and debate. Some organizations find it valuable to create off-site meetings around purpose. The intention of such gatherings is to find out what colleagues think. Leaders have influence over purpose but they do not define it nor sustain it. Only when employees embrace ownership of purpose will it matter."

Church security must focus on providing excellent customer service. Being prepared for emergency medical issues, church disrupters, etc. is all worthy; however the most interaction will be with congregants. These are opportunities to further the church mission and allow people to feel more safe and comfortable at the same time.

Kevin Robertson, Director of Security for Saddleback Church, wrote a book titled, "Church Security, Providing a Safe Worship Environment (2014). In the book, Robertson includes the Saddleback Church Security Ministry Purpose Statement:

"To provide a safe and secure environment for the children and adult members of Saddleback Church and the guests and visitors to ensure that their Saddleback experience is one that can focus on their spiritual growth and worship time, and to be as, "Wise as serpents and as gentle as doves."

To ensure as best as we can as disturbance-free of a worship experience as possible for those who come onto any of our campuses; if and when a disturbance does arise, our goal is to remove that disturbance in a Christ-like way and in a manner that is the very least attention-attracting to the situation as possible so that those attending the event go quickly back to focusing on why they are there. "

In a Harvard Business Review article by Grahm Kenny, Your Company's Purpose Is Not Its Vision, Mission, or Values – September 03, 2014, Kelly quoted Greg Ellis, former CEO and managing director of REA Group, who said, (purpose) "connects with the heart as well as the head. "

In our first team training, my personal purpose, our "why" and vision were shared with team members. Team members need to buy into the vision so that we are all on the same page.

Everyone on the team serves our Lord and Savior, Jesus Christ, first. We are blessed to share our gifts as we serve in this capacity of security for the church. I agree with Kevin Roberts who discusses each follower of Jesus Christ as a minister, to be taught by pastors, and I believe that that the worship security team is a ministry that allows us to help minister to those in need.

I love my church dearly. It has touched my heart and strengthens my soul. I have never known the Holy Spirit to move through me as I do now and my goal is to help further the mission of the church and to reach out to others. I am blessed to be volunteering in the security ministry with a committed and dedicated team that sacrifices much to serve with excellence. There is little doubt in my mind, that any one of us would forfeit ourselves to protect the congregation. I find this same commitment from individuals either on organized security teams or acting as security where no team exists in churches I have visited all over America.

So, we start with purpose. The following is from the SOGs prepared for my church and its satellite campuses: A full copy of the SOGs is available on our web site and in the appendix. Feel free to cut and paste them or to use them as a template for your team. Parts of other churches SOGs were researched and used to build our guides. The movement for better security, communications, and training has been based in open sharing.

We are continually looking for better policies and procedures and will rewrite or change our current guides when we find something better. There are several examples of this throughout the book. This book will have taken close to two years to complete before the first edition was ever printed. In that time, we have made quite a few changes.

Our goal isn't to show you a nice shiny polished apple. Understandably, each church has its own unique needs based upon individual risk assessments. Design your guidelines based upon your individual needs. Tweak the SOGs as necessary. More important is the discussion that takes place as teams are built and hopefully, this book lends to your discussions.

Purpose (From SOG)

Our church's Volunteer Security/EMS Team's (VST) purpose is to protect church employees, members, visitors, and property during church services, special events, and as requested, by serving as a real time threat assessment team and by providing pre planned/coordinated first response until outside agencies arrive. VST's focus is providing safety, security, and emergency medical help during church services inside church structures, and as requested.

Matthew 10:16 – "Behold, I send you out as sheep amongst wolves; therefore be as wise as serpents and harmless as doves."

How this verse applies to church security goals and objectives is "wise as serpents" instructs us to "prepare in advance" and "harmless as doves" instructs us to "do so in a Christ-like way that complements our church's "CORE MISSION" ... to lead people into a fully-devoted relationship with Jesus Christ by loving people, cultivating community, and inspiring hope."

"Our Church's VST program objectives are to use Deter, Detect, Delay, and Deny as the model through which we will achieve our goals. The VST will respond to and recover from related events and assist with basic emergency medical services. We achieve this through creation of SOGs, proper vetting of volunteer safety personnel, training, and building relationships with local emergency providers, other worship safety/security teams, and the community. The VST, under the direction of church leadership, is committed to this program to positively impact the mission of our church.

Our mission is to help assure our Church is a safe place where those who are seeking can find salvation through our Lord and Savior Jesus Christ.

Scope

Scope is an essential aspect of a project needed to develop a common understanding of what is included in and excluded from the project. The scope builds upon the project concept developed in the conception stage, sets limits, and defines roles.

Scope is usually defined by:
Project Need
Project Goals
Product Description
Project Customer, Sponsor, Manager
Project Critical Success Factors
Project Assumptions
Project Constraints
Project Deliverables
Project Rationale/Purpose

Defining a project's scope helps establish a common understanding for all project stakeholders. It is the foundation on which the schedule, budget and staffing plans are built.

Defining the scope accurately, may require the implementation of a safety and security assessment.

"How To Assess the Safety and Security of Your Place of Worship," By: Tina Lewis Rowe (2009) defines a security risk assessment in relation to defining the scope:

"Prior to defining the scope, your church may decide to perform a security risk analysis. A security assessment is an inspection of a person, place, asset, process or program, to evaluate the current condition of safety, security and preparedness for an emergency. It considers risks, sources and nature of threats and criticality of harm. It considers the factors that would enable prevention, deterrence, protection, detection, resistance and response.

A thorough security assessment will include reviewing and inspecting: Safety (accidents, illness, injuries, potential harm to people or the organization.) Security (crimes, violence, loss or damage from any cause) Emergency Preparedness (response and recovery related to any harmful event or situation of any kind—including plans to be a resource for assistance if an emergency occurs in the community), Continuity planning (Preparedness to continue services and programs without significant interruption), The overall status of each component of a safe and secure place of worship, (Anything related to the place of worship or its assets and activities that can be inspected, reviewed, inventoried or evaluated, as designated by church leaders.)"

"The Ministry of Defense; Executive Protection for the Ministry," by: Pablo Birriel (2006) suggests it is, "...In your best interest to think like an attacker."

Identify blind spots and areas of opportunity for potential threats. Know your physical exposures, i.e. tithe collection areas, money and/or product transport, parking lots, etc. When our church's Administration building was built, the architect included a wheelchair accessible ramp on the right side of the front entrance. There is a wall along the ramp that snakes its way from the main walk to the entrance. On the opposite side of the entrance is a small tree, surrounded by a similar type wall that certainly could provide good cover for someone who knew our offerings transport rout and wanted to surprise the transporters. By identifying this, we become more aware and instruct anyone involved with the transport to look at window reflections as they approach. Some fixes to bind spots can be very inexpensive.

"Keeping Your Church Safe," by: Ron Aguiar (2008) is also an exceptional resource. Other services may be available to help you identify risk, including: Department of Homeland Security, FBI, local police and fire departments, your church's insurance company, outside businesses that specialize in church security and some church security associations.

Your insurance company may provide a resource for risk assessments. Brotherhood Mutual (brotherhoodmutual.com) has an excellent church security resource section available online. Click on the "Resources" tab, and you'll see "Safety and Risk Management for Ministries," which offers a wealth of information. They also have a "Church Safety & Security Guidebook," which can be ordered online for under $50.00. From 2016, when this book was initiall written through 2017, I have found a lot of agencies, companies, nonprofits, associations, and individuals willing to help churches stay safe.

Always remember, bad guys get into the areas they seek by acting like good guys. This trait is also what will make them stick out and be easier to detect, more on that later. Bad guys have goals that good guys don't typically think about, because good guy's hearts are more pure. Something simple like designing an aesthetic entrance to your building may actually provide an opportunity for someone who has different goals. Good guys shouldn't pretend that they are capable of seeing all potential risks, which is why experts will be the best source for risk assessments.

Just a note: Most threats will be men (over 91% as of 2016), though some teens, women, and even children can also pose risk to your church. The same is true of security teams, while women do volunteer on security teams, it is mostly males and thus I refer to shepherds and threats as guys. There is no offense intended. Women are encouraged to participate on our teams and are actively recruited just as the men in our congregation are.

By the way…this past December (2016) two of our tithe boxes were broken into during a very crowded event. Video surveillance showed it was a younger woman in her early 20's who artfully bent the tops of the metal box by slamming her hand into the corner f the box and pushing up. She was very efficient at doing this all while holding her 2 year old in her other arm.

SCOPE (From SOGs)

"The scope of the VST is limited to the activities inside the church for a short period of time prior to worship services, during worship services, time between services, for a short period of time after services and includes special events like speakers and productions held on the Church premises as requested. VST may also provide services outside of buildings, including off campus events as requested. EMS team members are not required to perform security functions, but may do so, if they choose."

Some churches may decide the scope of security functions includes a children's center, parking lot, or entire campus. Our SOGs are fluid and open for adjustment. Teams will expand and contract over time. Scope should be flexible enough to expand and contract with the team's capabilities and the needs of the church.

Volunteers run into scheduling conflicts all the time. Their children get sick. Deserved vacations are taken. Medical issues arise. Sometimes finances force team members to work extra hours or take on additional jobs. Family needs and events occur. I'm sure you've heard all the reasons why someone missed church. And, when that person is part of a ministry that performs a function at church, like greeters or ushers, that role may not be able to go unfilled.

Now start multiplying that out – three ushers miss church on the same day, for the same service. Just because servants don't show up doesn't mean the job doesn't have to get done – it still does. Open positions need to be filled.

It is very easy to ask the person already sitting in the church doing security to help out. They're there now…it only takes a couple of minutes…nothing is happening right now anyway…you see where this is going. The faithful servant can't say no. Many times the person who volunteers for the security team came from ushers and they already know the job and empathize with the need.

Please remember a few things: The bad guy gets into our circle of confidence by acting like the good guy. Bad guy is not always a stranger. And, bad guy is always looking for opportunity, like when a person volunteering for security team duty is asked to fill in for someone who didn't show up and leaves their assigned post of protection to pass a bucket.

Usually, it's "when" not "if" – a security person is asked to perform a duty that pulls them off their post. Even when a security person isn't being tapped on the shoulder to help out in some way, all it may take for a threat to penetrate or escalate is that opportunity presented in that moment, where attention has been diverted, like doing an usher's job of quieting a baby, greeting and seating people, etc.

To many readers, this may sound crazy, but we schedule according to the Holy Spirit, especially during events outside of regular services. When we follow the Holy Spirit, we are always in the right place at the right time. If we miss something – it was supposed to be missed and vice versa.

During our annual Christmas production, over 70,000 people walked through our doors. Without a schedule, we had every show covered with security and EMS. Team members asked for a schedule continually. The response always was, "If the Holy Spirit moves you to be here, be here. If the Spirit moves you otherwise, do what you have to do."

That last line is probably the strongest message we can send. After all, who among us that wants to serve would deny the Holy Spirit? Very powerful.

Security team pre and post service assignments are determined by defining vulnerabilities, providing a perimeter cover that will defend them, and training the volunteers their role in that assignment. Again, it's hard for "Good guys" to imagine the thought pattern of every bad guy, though we sometimes believe that we have walked in their shoes, or came close enough to empathize. But the person who is there to do harm may notice the breach of protocol, or the hole in protection, and may find opportunity to use it to their advantage. When the breach occurs, and the system dynamics have changed, due to the loss of control at that position, other security and the church could be at greater risk, as all response plans are determined with the belief and understanding that everyone will be in their assigned position.

Sharing stories about our learning curve, my goal is to demonstrate the differences between a planned and trained team and a bunch of compassionate guys who meet at church services ready to protect the flock. Yes, the teams or individuals who lived through a gruesome attack have a story that we need to hear, but I am hard pressed to think of a church where the worst case scenario has happened twice. Thank you Lord for your hand that protects us, most of us have never had to face the threat of deadly violence. But, we still have disrupters, people who seek to take what is not theirs, EMS calls, etc., and I believe there is opportunity to learn from others mistakes.

Little things will always happen on a volunteer team. It is better to make mistakes in training and we can expose weaknesses in training to share with everyone on the team so we can all learn from them.

When we were looking at writing our first SOGs, we developed a procedure for positioning the team. Almost half of the positions required that the team member who took that assignment couldn't leave their post to respond to a disturbance anywhere else in the church. In the beginning, I had more than one team member tell me they took on two roles: they performed security at very crucial position assignments, and they also helped with ushering. At least half of our disruptions came from these assigned areas. I used to get nervous when team members would leave their post to perform usher duties and would bring it up with the person who was doing it in a private conversation. It did not go away on its own. Change is hard. Expect that. Look for opportunities to use mistakes in training and be patient with you team. Again, we're always in the right place at the right time.

During one service, someone from our outside team made a radio announcement that there was a man with a gun. No other information. No location, no additional radio communication. Radio communications with that person were attempted, but there was no response. We wanted to know where this person was. Our campus is over 10 buildings on 72 acres. For all we knew, this security person could be lying on the ground dead and the shooter could be making their way into the church.

It turned out to be a man with the gun was a regular church attendee and was open carrying a pistol into church. This is perfectly legal in Arizona; we don't have any signage restricting it, though we do ask that people conceal their weapon. He was one of our pastor's brothers, but no one on the inside security team inside knew that. The person was asked to conceal the weapon or put it in his car and he complied immediately, but it took many minutes to find out that there was no threat.

Two volunteer security team members who were assigned to watch the stairs to the stage – a critical position that only responds to protect the pastor, left their positions to do something, I don't know what, in a place where we weren't sure where it was, for a situation we knew little about. We are not cowboys riding out on a posse, ready to do battle wherever we find it. We provide security in a specific manner with detailed plans. When they left their positions, their areas of responsibility were totally open.

When these team members came back, they were shown the gap in protection. It can be very sobering to see what consequences may have been, and a huge blessing that there was no secondary threat inside the service.

Every team will have its quirks. Team building may mean accepting these peculiarities and developing them. Veteran team members tend to establish themselves by claiming something that belongs to the team. The fire department I served with owned a large track of property titled, "Fireman's Park." Firefighters were instructed to volunteer at the park every week. It was a huge property big enough to host our County's fair.

Chores were posted and people coming to help picked their task and crossed it off the list. Think about similar situations in your church. Envision the process and you should be able to see the veteran servants doing their preferred job and leaving the dirtier or odd jobs to the newer people hoping to serve. When leaders allow this to happen, they may be promoting a kind of good-old-boys club mentality. When opportunities are limited or restricted based on habits or desires, it could negatively affect the team.

We'll cover this in more detail later in the book, but I believe the greater takeaway is the effect it has on volunteers, teams, and leadership development. There are several things we are instituting to encourage different behavior like, recruiting enough security personnel so that any one person would only have to perform security functions at one service a week, and creating a sign in sheet that details the most important positions first and forcing the first person who signs in to take that first position. We encourage leadership compelling team members to know every position and the responsibilities that go along with them and in training we rotate people in different positions after every scenario.

Additionally, some people planning to disrupt a service may scope out the facility in advance of executing their plan. Having the same person at the same position every service may offer a predictable weakness. And, when a team member is always in the same place, they become less aware of their surroundings.

I include this to show that security is never as perfect as we would like or plan. It gets very close. There are several things we are implementing to overcome this "comfort thing." Since "excellence" is our goal, we determine scope to define and limit personal choices, range of opportunity, and set boundaries that help us achieve our primary goals.

Goals

Team goals are as follows: Recruit, train, and operate a security/EMS team that will focus on the safety and security of the church before, during, and after worship services on church grounds or as requested for other church functions, and offer certified responders for medical emergencies.

Inside our team, our goals are to offer fraternity to members and to rely on each other in our walk with Christ Jesus. We seek to build leaders and give purpose to those who sacrifice their time and talents and to serve by seeking excellence in mission and vision.

Team members will be assigned to specific pastors and will accept position assignments to assure their safety. Risks and responses will be detailed in training.

VST's primary focus is the safety of pastors and will always be a primary consideration. As more safety team members arrive, the scope and perimeter of coverage may expand to include: people attending worship, children, church property and assets, protection against liability, and EMS response.

As church campuses are added to our church's list, duplication of these SOGs and training to other campuses should be easy. The goal would be to have all campuses on the same page with the VST and to establish clear communications and predictable response.

***

Please remember, these SOGs are written for the Volunteer Security/EMS Team. At our church, there are a few levels of security besides the volunteer team. We have identifiable paid security employees who are on site 24/7, uniformed police, parking lot or outside security, and ushers/greeters who are not security, but are observing congregants and are trained to assess people that don't look right, or cause their trust radar to alert them, and they notify us to respond.

These "goals," as with the SOGs, only pertain to the church's volunteer security team only. We seek mutual efforts, but do not impose our SOGs on any other group.

Writing goals will be easier after a risk assessment has been completed.

Successful achievement of goals can be measured. We have established a security ministry specifically because threats from individuals cannot be predicted and so it is our measured response to threats and interruptions that is considered and assessed.

Choosing the church pastor as the prime focus gives us a starting place as we define security goals. The strength of the pastor to achieve church mission, vision, and goals, raise necessary funds to achieve success, and motivate long time members as well as new people seeking God's glory that redemption brings. Our pastor and his family are amazing as is his deep commitment to the church mission and his outstanding vision for growth. Without him, I'm sure people would step up, but we can't imagine the perfect flow of energy and appeal that he has mastered easily being easily transferred. Thus, he is our most important focus.

Most of the time we're dealing with service disrupters. Sometimes, these people just sit in their seats, sometimes they stand and yell, but once in a great while there is a very real threat. By focusing on one primary person, we can stage security in places that also allow us to view the entire audience. Peripheral vision is usually more effective than direct eye contact at spotting a need. It allows us to respond to any situation, while still maintaining focus on our primary objective.

As more volunteer security team members show up, our perimeter and coverage abilities increase. At the time I began writing this book, we had a goal of growing our team by two hundred percent, or tripling the size. After attending a few national security seminars and participating in security discussions with other church security leaders, the goal was changed to a 600% increase or multiplying the current team size by seven - more on this in Chapter Three.

Known "risks" could be people with a past history. We welcome and acknowledge that our goal is to help everyone find the Lord through His Son Jesus Christ, so we want everyone to come and participate. Even people who may be asked to leave today may be encouraged to come back at another time. Expanding coverage also includes increasing outreach - a subject that gets its own heading in this chapter.

In a weekly team communication, I wrote the following and believe this is exactly what our duty is:

Matthew 5:9 "Blessed are the peacemakers, for they shall be called sons of God." Peace is found in our commitment to God through Christ Jesus, and is felt when we accept direction through the Holy Spirit. Those of us who feel compelled to protect the Lord's flock are blessed with this opportunity through our church. It is therefore incumbent upon each of us to step up to the plate and offer the best we are capable of.

Matthew 5:44 "But I say to you, Love your enemies and pray for those who persecute you." This one single line I believe explains exactly how we, as a volunteer security team, are to fulfill our duties. When we deter someone who may be a threat, there is no judgment. We love everyone and pray for those whose intentions may be against us. Detecting a person who does not fit the baseline is an observation – not a judgment. This is an important distinction, because without exact definition, it is too easy to blur our purpose, which is to protect.

Matthew 6:13 "…but deliver us from evil." This is the last line of the Lord's Prayer. God uses people to achieve His will. It is incumbent upon us to have the ability to respond when evil invades our church. Response should be planned, trained, and implemented according to our purpose and goals, which are based in our church's doctrine.

Team growth allows additional coverage to smaller services or services held outside of the Wednesday/Sunday timeframe. Adding a bicycle patrol in the parking lots, having additional outside security, covering more events, etc., are all goals of our team and endless recruiting makes it all possible.

Within the past couple of years, our church has added four additional campuses and seeks even greater reach. More campuses are coming. Our pastor's bigger goal is to have Arizona referred to as the "Christian State," and he sees his goal being achieved through large growth. Multiple campus churches are not unique in the metro Phoenix area.

Our church plans are to continue adding satellite churches throughout the state. Goals with the security ministry SOGs include a duplicable plan that other campuses can adopt and easily initiate. It allows us to have all campuses train as one unit, which also provides a means of introduction between team members, sharing of experience, needs, and ideas. An unwritten goal is to be able to have security team members fill in at other churches as requested and to be familiar with their lay out and operations.

If we can use these SOGs to duplicate excellent service at our church campuses, certainly you can utilize them at your church too.

***

Excellence is a process of trial and error and most important is the deep faith and true belief that everything will happen in God's time. Patience is a virtue, and given time, input from other successful ministries, commitment and dedication from church leaders and team members, everything usually falls into place the way it's supposed to.

Implementing standard operating procedures and training them to our team is a key element to our team's success. We began a monthly training, initially set for Saturday morning. Some team members could not attend for one reason or another. So, we instituted training on Thursday night alternating between the two satellite campuses, along with our set training on Saturday morning.

Thursday night did not work and it was scrapped. We are currently looking into recording training events and offering them to team members through the church website.

The goal is to have more people trained in every aspect of worship service security, to train as professionals whose desire is to provide a safe environment, where people can hear our pastor speaking God's Word to strengthen their beliefs and understanding. We strive for the best possible results at every service. It's also important that we develop new leaders who will take over and build on the foundation we create.

"Six Sigma" is a set of techniques and tools for process improvement. It was introduced by engineer Bill Smith while working at Motorola in 1986. Jack Welch made it central to his business strategy at General Electric in 1995. Today, it is used in many industrial and other business sectors. In 2005 Motorola attributed over $17 billion in savings to Six Sigma.

For our purposes, the system works off an acronym **RDMAIC**:

- **R**ecognize the right problem
- **D**efine the system and the project goals
- **M**easure key aspects of the current process and collect relevant data
- **A**nalyze the data to investigate and verify cause-and-effect relationships Determine what the relationships are, attempt to ensure that all factors have been considered, seek out root cause of the defect under investigation

- Improve or optimize the current process based upon data analysis
- Control - Implement control systems and continuously monitor the process

Example: Our first training was on a Saturday morning. While we had a good attendance, about 1/3 of the team was unable to attend. We made introductions, trained on basics, answered questions, drew out some diagrams, and had a pizza lunch.

Next morning, first service was at 9:00am. Every team member who was at the church was also at training the day before. Second service was at 11:00am. But this time, only two of us had been at the training.

The comments I got from that from the pastor responsible for our "First Impressions" team that oversees ushers, greeters, and church appearance on that day were, "First service was tight. I could feel it." Followed by, "Second service…not so much."

Recognizing the right problem can be the toughest part. In the example above, people could literally feel the difference among the team between the two services. So, this time, it was a bit easier to "Recognize" the right problem. Training vs. veteran experience only was the biggest difference between the two services. The first team had attended training and was on the same page, while veterans weren't so eager to train and fell back on old habits that we wanted to change. Change starts with vision, is written in SOGs, and is communicated at meetings and training events.

Defining the system and goals is also easy. Everyone needs to know and work through the SOGs, the expectation is top shelf professionalism and team members need to know how to communicate, how to identify threats, and how to react – including backing up fellow team members. It's all in the SOGs.

Remember – if it isn't written – it doesn't exist.

Measuring key aspects of the current condition was also easy. People other than me noticed it and made comments. Since we could compare "Tight team" to "Loose team," and since we knew who attended the only training we offered, the apparent opportunity was in trying to offer more training times.

Analyzing is a process of gathering information. This too can be a fairly simple process. It was as easy as asking the team members who missed the Saturday training if Thursday at 6:30 would be a better time and if they had a preference as to which campus we would like to meet at. However, other alternatives were suggested, such as videotaping the training.

Improving the current process was as simple as initiating a second training day. When that failed, the process was revisited and the added training was canceled after three attempts and no takers.

What we realized was that no matter what we offered, some of the veteran team members would not respond to any training opportunity. Typically, these team members will eventually rotate out as new team members come in or they eventually adapt to our program.

Control – monitoring the process, we will see gradual improvement in professionalism and response. Based upon other books regarding church security, some writers have indicated they experience a slight flow of comments, letters, and posts from congregants about their appreciation for a more professional and helpful security presence.

Again, it starts with goals. If the goal is simply to have Fred, the retired police officer in your congregation standing by the back door to look over everyone and pat down every new person who comes into the church – that is exactly what you will have. Eventually, Fred will leave for one reason or another and someone will assume his position. That person, unlike Fred, isn't really trained – only the new person won't ever be as smooth as Fred was. Making your goal to be the best you can be within your means is crucial to a successful security program.

At a meeting of security directors in Phoenix's East Valley, Mark Fritts, (group leader), offered this amazing question: On a scale of 1 -10, with 1 being nonexistent and 10 being the best, where do you rate your security team right now?

Regardless of your answer, we will find there is always room for improvement. These opportunities for improvement can be tackled at training events and/or team meetings. Identify the specific concern or risk you believe is lacking. Allow input from the team and other community support and do some research. Maybe someone else who solved the same problem has some good input. Try the idea(s) you believe fits your team best. Over time, reevaluate. Is the new process working better? Always shoot for excellence!

Touch

Achieving the goals of the church, excellent customer service has got to be a priority. One of the areas where the security team can help is in the "touch" process. "Touch" is a marketing term that became popular in about 2013.

In a blog post by LMD@LisaMarieDiasDesigns.com, 7 TOUCHES – A BASIC "MARKETING PRINCIPLE IN ACTION, posted 10th Apr 2013, the author writes:

"It is a basic marketing principle that it takes seven 'touches' before someone will internalize and/or act upon your call to action. These touches can take many forms:

- A physical connection, such as meeting at a networking event
- Seeing an ad, either physical or digital
- Seeing your logo, maybe as a sponsor or on a brochure
- Seeing your social media posts in a news stream
- Receiving your e-newsletter or other email marketing piece
- A phone call
- A Word of Mouth mention by a friend or colleague"

Our First Impressions leader has set up a system of personal "touches" for church services. There are other "touch" marketing techniques in place, but this is about the personal "touch" and how the worship security team plays a role.

Touch one - Driving into the parking lot, lot attendants and golf cart drivers are identifiable; they should offer a cheerful wave to people entering the lots and greet them as they walk from their cars to the main walkway. When cart drivers drop people off, they are courteous and offer joyful welcomes.

Touch two - At the tip of the main walk is another greeter, someone who can answer questions.

Touch three – is a greeter at the door.

Touch four – is a pastor greeting guests, separate from the volunteer greeters.

Touch five – A pair of greeters inside the building offer service programs.

Touch six – people walk past a welcoming desk where they can fill out or drop off "Get Connected" cards and are greeted again.

Touch seven – Ushers welcome people to services and guide them to open seats, answer questions, and assist anyone with special needs.

There it is - seven touches.

As we will discuss later in the book, greeters, ushers, pastors, volunteers, and congregants are our first line of deterrence and detection. We invite them to our security training when we train on awareness twice annually, so we can utilize their abilities to help us detect someone who just doesn't look right. It makes sense that the church should be able to count on us to utilize our abilities to increase the effectiveness of the seven touches. And we want volunteers to feel comfortable alerting us when someone they encounter causes an emotional threat alert.

Part of our desire for excellent customer service must be to make sure congregants, volunteers, and staff feels and knows we are accessible to them. To achieve this, security team members are assigned to main entrances before, during, and in-between services. They are trained to smile and greet people entering the building.

Formerly, the security team kept a separated mission attitude, which is certainly understandable. Many churches have expressed fear of security teams acting like jack booted thugs and creating an atmosphere not conducive to the goals of the church, which again is understandable. Hopefully, what we are demonstrating here is that having a written policy that aligns mission with church, that depends upon and includes other missions, volunteers, staff, and congregants, we can help further the goals of the church and the security team.

We acknowledge that we cannot be everywhere all the time. Even video surveillance systems sometimes experience human and technical errors. It certainly is comforting to be able to rely on others to help keep the church safe.

Chapter 3

DEVELOPING THE TEAM

Developing the team requires vision. Painting the picture of where you want to go and what everything should look like means defining the present. We already discussed risk assessments and now we're going to move coverage out to encompass more of church the property. Vision includes using measurements to plan for the future by assessing what present and future concerns could be.

Protecting Your Church Against Mass Violence, 18 Jun, 2015 in The Pen tagged Church / church violence / JD Hall / security / shooting / violence by JD Hall

"Statistics (from 1999 to February of 2015) demonstrate 971 "deadly force incidents" in churches or faith-based operations. Of those, only about 200 incidents are from people who knew each other (friends or relatives) doing violence upon each other. The rest are outside-in incidents. Only about 47 of those incidents were religion based (so called "hate crimes") and 576 of those incidents included firearms. Of these incidents, 375 occurred during "service" hours and the rest during off-hours.

These incidents have been on the rise in America, beginning in 1980 when a gunman shouted, "This is war!" and began to shoot up First Baptist Church in Dangerfield, Texas – killing five and wounding ten more. Since then, on-grounds church violence has been a normal occurrence, although it doesn't make the international news in the same way as this seemingly race-motivated murder spree yesterday."

According to Hartford Institute for Religion Research, as of 2010 there were approx. 300,000 churches in the US and about 56 million congregants attending them. Simple math will show the potential for a deadly force incident at any given church to be about a .0002 percent chance or less in any given year (971 incidents over 16 years at 300,000 churches). The point is, while I do believe that we have to be prepared for the worst, the brunt of our responses will be addressing threats to disrupt and EMS calls. Thus it is important that security teams have the ability to assess threats, deter disruptions from happening, detect EMS needs and other events that are out of the baseline of normal church service, deny threats or disturbances from growing, respond to events until outside agencies arrive, and help recover from loss events.

Carl Chinn compiled a report that includes the following Statistics on violence in faith-based organizations in 2014: (go to carlchin.com for updates).

- 176 deadly force incidents were documented at churches and faith-based organizations in the US. This passed the highest figures on violence from 2012 by 37 incidents, a jarring 21 percent increase. Last year also saw a near record total violent deaths: 74.
- 52 of the 74 violent deaths (70 percent) were innocent victims. The other 22 deaths (30 percent), were suicides or perpetrators killed in the act.
- There were 14 suicides. Unfortunately, 8 other victims died at the hand of those committing their own suicide.
- There were 24 incidents in which the pastor or priest of the church was directly involved. Of those leaders, 6 died in the altercation or committed suicide.
- 18.2 percent of incidents were relayed to domestic violence.
- 26.8 percent were robberies.
- 29 of the attackers were somehow associated with the church.

Carl Chinn became an early expert in church security, but not by choice. He was first indelibly touched by a violent incident at his church in 1996. According to Sara Horn, Freelance writer living in Nashville; visit sara-horn.com (www.947krks.com/11605335/#sthash.jUeSWGPh.dpuf) – "A man who had been permanently injured while working as a construction worker when the Colorado offices for Focus (Focus on the Family) were being built had taken two women in the front lobby hostage and was threatening to blow up the building. Because of the ministry's quick security response, effective law enforcement tactics and prayer, the man was ultimately convinced by police to release the hostages and eventually taken into custody. But for Chinn, if security had not been at the forefront of his mind before, it certainly was now."

Reality struck Mr. Chinn again in December 2007, when another shooter appeared at the church. This time two young women were shot in front of their parents as the gunman set his stage for what could have been a much worse scenario. But the churches security team, under Chinn's direction, had adopted policies and procedures that were engrained in the heads of all team members. To hear Carl talk about the 1996 incident is incredible. Lightning should never strike twice, but for Carl it did and to see him reveal step-by-step the movements and incidents of the second scenario in 2007 is surreal.

According to a Police Magazine article (04/05/2012) 5 Ways to Prevent Crime Against Churches – Basic security measures can keep many such crimes from occurring so you won't need to investigate them, by Jeffrey A. Hawkins writes, "The problem of churches and crime is not going away. As the rest of society adopts better security measures, unless churches follow suit they will become an increasingly appealing opportunity for criminals of all kinds. Thirty years ago law enforcement had very few security concerns about churches, but as society changes, all houses of worship will face increasing threats and the need for greater law enforcement attention."

At a Sheepdog Seminar in Phoenix AZ, Lt. Colonel Dave Grossman spoke about the dangers of video game violence to America's youth. He cites a general increase in violence akin to a wave that is not going away.

We focus on statistics that generally identify the worst periods of violence. While Chicago experienced its worst homicide rate in many decades (2016), violent crimes soared as well. Media wanted us to focus on the gun violence and rarely talked about the increase in violent crimes overall. The point being; security teams are not just about active shooters and terrorist threats.

Through strict adherence of SOGs and training, we can teach volunteer security team members how to respond in a way that is geared to help protect them, the church, and other congregants. I haven't found a way to teach true empathy and compassion to individuals, which will be the key to many more successful responses our churches will face. Personally, I'm looking for Christians who have it in their heart to serve in a Christ-Like way. A lot of empathy and compassion goes a long way to resolving conflicts and yet, our teams must also know set steps designed to protect themselves and the church, should de-escalation efforts not work.

Set guidelines regarding who may serve on the team need to be in place and followed. Background checks and interviews must be conducted. More about these things will be covered later in this chapter.

We train our team to deter potential threats first. We do this by making our presence known, with identifiers that congregants can easily see and understand why we are here. Our goal is to be obvious, but not over bearing. Our presence is not meant to intimidate, it's meant to reassure. I'm not as concerned about a team member's ability to defend themselves, as much as their ability to back up another team member according to our SOGs. Sometimes, having the appearance of larger numbers is enough to de-escalate a situation that otherwise might have gotten a challenge if it was only a one-on-one situation. We're not looking for people whose goal is to prove themselves to others. I'm not interested in "wanna-be" cops who couldn't pass a psychiatric evaluation and thus, didn't get into the police academy, but find it easier to join a church security group. Brains overrule muscles and preferably applicants have both.

Experience is a great asset, but not all people with experience are great additions. Your church security program has to have a solid foundation with leaders who will assure the security program is in place long after they are gone from the team.

There is a team in my community comprised of retired police officers. The leader is at least 70 years old and has been retired from the department for at least 15 years. Yes, he is a man of God. Yes, he has compassion in his heart. But his team is limited to guessing at response, because nothing is in writing. While he may know exactly what he is doing, he has no means of training others or breeding leaders.

These officers on this team are from all over the US. Their training, experience, job description, and job performance are all different. One of the firefighters I served with was an overzealous person who used his fire department badge and red emergency dashboard light to pull people over in their cars and issue them warnings. He was a hazard to himself and everyone on the team. His service was about him.

Wisconsin winters can have some very cold nights. There are two kinds of ice, that which you can see and that which is so glassy, it's almost invisible. I was the line officer for a nighttime apartment fire and the two of us had the responsibility of providing the backup line – as specified in SOGs – to support the first team on the attack line. So there is a plan.

We were on the first out attack truck, which was four-wheel drive. I normally take the large step from the cab to the ground, but slipped onto may back (where my air tank was) and was laying on the ground. I couldn't easily get up. Then the guy on my team looked out of the cab and jumped onto my ankles, breaking one. He proceeded, by himself, to go into the burning building without a hose or a tool. This is a guy I probably don't want on my team.

Again, his service was all about him. The team fighting the fire did not have the backup they expected. His selfishness left me lying on the ground, forcing an EMS team to help me, and pulling them from attending another patient. And, the ambulance that transported me to the hospital was now out of service.

I'm going to cite Gavin De Becker in this chapter twice. In his book, The Gift of Fear – Survival Signals That Protect Us From Violence (1997), Gavin provides insight of how people can use fear to their advantage. It tells us when something doesn't feel right. We will be discussing tactical approaches to security in the chapter on "Training" and again in "Operations."

Awareness is the key to successfully identifying and defusing most situations. Team members must be able to communicate with congregants, over radio communications, with church staff, and with outside agencies who may be called in to help with a situation like EMS or a drunken disorderly. Communications, mainly, are our method of causing the threat to delay and allowing time for team backup and/or outside agency response.

Gavin also suggests that children who have been abused sexually, physically, or mentally make great detectors. They grow up learning to read their predators facial expressions and can sense danger. However, I don't imagine that we will ever see a question on a ministry application asking about someone's childhood abuse, but it is an interesting point.

Trust your instincts when interviewing potential team members. Don't be afraid to have a probationary period. Since our team is larger, we have team leaders for each service. I rely on them to report anything out of place with a team member and also to discuss those who should be put on a leadership track.

Entering church one day, greeters told me that a new congregant wanted to join our security team. Before I knew who that person was, I reported a person of interest sitting immediately behind our pastors. You can imagine my surprise when both were the same person.

It was apparent that volunteers and staff felt uncomfortable with this person, just as I did.

We had a brief interview where I found that this person wanted to serve with the Children's Ministry and with security. I felt this 36 year old, single male wanted a position of authority to lure children away. He never got the opportunity…not that he didn't try over and over again for months.

Probably the most important element we're looking for can be found in Kevin Robertson's book, "Church Security – Providing a Safe Worship Service." Saddleback Church supports the belief that every person is a minister of God and that it's the pastor's job to teach the congregant how to minister. The goal is to bring people closer to God and Jesus Christ and we are here to minister to those God puts before us.

Robertson writes, "When we recruit team members, we're flexible in some areas, but in two specific areas, we're not. First, everyone we interact with will be treated in a Christ-like way - - it's all about grace." "Second, they need to be comfortable praying with someone."

Since reading his book, we have encouraged our team to praying with people in their time of need. But it's not just any people. We train to look for the people we are suspicious of (doesn't look right/people of interest) and reach out. What an amazing opportunity! First, we get to make contact with someone, which also means we can ask questions and get a better gauge on our suspicions. Many times, people are just waiting to be asked something and they are willing to open up with their stories. This is where empathy and compassion come into play. This is exactly why the Christ-like heart is important. If a team member is just playing, if they are not truthful, or led by the Holy Spirit someone else will sense that right away.

During one service I was roaming in the outer sanctuary area across from where the uniformed police officer was standing. A young homeless guy walked up to the officer and started mumbling something about needing to go get something. The cop realized almost immediately that something wasn't right.

As the guy zigged towards me, I reached out and gently took his arm. Looking into his eyes I politely asked if he needed anything. He told me he had to go pick up his mother and gave a reason that sounded weird, and then asked where the bathroom was. It really didn't matter, so I decided it wasn't worth assessing any further. Then he offered that he was homeless and was staying at a shelter run by the church. I confided in him and prayed with him. Then he let me know he really wasn't picking up his mother, he just wanted to go outside and smoke. Not that any of this is a big deal, except that maybe on this day he was able to get a little closer to our pastor's message and just maybe he found a Christian who shared something personal, treated him with dignity and respect, and helped him find God's amazing grace.

Acts of violence are typically not something that happens all of a sudden.

It is a process everyone goes through. De Becker describes the process of violence by likening it to a ladder. No one just shows up one day and starts shooting. It begins with a thought based upon a perception. Triggers may increase anger and the threat takes another step up the ladder. He imagines himself disrupting a service and takes another step up. Eventually, he wakes up one morning, takes a shower, eats breakfast, puts his pistol in his belt, gets in his car and drives to church. Once he gets there, he looks for a parking space, walks in, says hi to everyone along the way and finds a seat. He may even participate in worship and tithing. Them he sees the object of his anger. He reaches for his gun, taking yet another step up the ladder. And with each additional rung he climbs, he gets closer and closer to his imagined revenge.

At any point in the climb up the ladder, the threat may be able to be deterred, detected, or delayed. Sometimes it can be as simple as a security team member asking if everything is OK. Maybe, it's the willingness to pray with that person that de-escalates the threat. One thing is certain, if we fail to act or over react, we cannot go back and start over.

Experience is also a good qualifier; though I personally wouldn't create a situation where only having experience is the team guideline. Social Media recruiting posts and church bulletin notices I've seen for security team members typically advertise for police, fire, EMS, and military experience. While these people may have experience in high stress environments, I believe that we can train none-experienced people who want to serve and even develop them into leaders.

Equal opportunity for everyone should also be a concern, as violations of this are not only unethical, they could be a liability to the church.

Team Membership SOG

1.1 Membership

1. Any church member, who has been at your church for at least six (6) months, may apply to the VST for membership. We seek people who have the most important ingredients of all, those being: a shepherd's heart, integrity, commitment to a task and

people skills. Any member with less than six months at the church must receive the approval of VST leaders.

EMS volunteers must be a currently licensed CNA, EMT, Paramedic, Nurse, or Physician.

2. All potential VST members must complete the church volunteer application and complete a background check. Background checks to include criminal checks in all 50 states, employment and reference checks. These checks will be completed on all team members at least every two years or as requested.

3. After successfully passing the background check, the applicant will be interviewed by one or more of the following: the Security Team Director, Assistant Team Director, church leader and/or security team member designated by the VST Director.

4. Volunteers must be able to attend (8) eight of (11) eleven scheduled training sessions, including (1) one mandatory full day training (1) one time annually and meet other commitments. If a volunteer will be driving vehicles owned by your church or any of its affiliates, a Motor Vehicle Check should be obtained. Church leadership may determine acceptable number of accidents, violations, and types that are acceptable.

EMS volunteers must provide a copy of their current certifications, are responsible for maintaining their certifications, and must provide copies of certifications at least annually. Any EMS volunteer that loses certification or is past their renewal deadline must notify the VST EMS leader. Only volunteers with current certification may participate as a VST member.

5. Removal from the VST will occur to any member found providing false information on their application or background check, or who willfully hides pertinent information. Misconduct, abuse of power, failure to follow the mission of the team or the church or fulfilling responsibilities, and/or the inability to work as VST member are reasons for removal.

Any team member who does not participate or communicate

their reason for absence longer than (3) three consecutive months will be removed from the team roster. Any team member who is dropped or removed from the list may reapply and must complete a new background check.

Recruiting
Very simply put, the act of recruiting means, enlisting new people, in our case it is volunteers. Some churches may not need to attract many new security people or they may be like our team, looking to expand to seventy eight team members over three campuses. Define your needs and your desires first.

When I joined this team, there were about six security team members. We were forced to staff security with fewer people than necessary to achieve our goals. A few existing team members would attend three of the five services, leaving two totally without security. Many attended only the two Sunday services, and the midweek service was definitely understaffed. We sometimes staffed our security with only two or three members.

We decided that we wanted enough people on the team to staff all five services throughout the week, without having to count on anyone having to attend more than one service.

During the recruiting process every prospect would ask what the expectations were. People who make commitments like to know what their commitment is up front and surely every person reading this can relate to the efforts needed to attract and retain volunteers. The new "desire" was to have one team in place for each service and have each team member only responsible for one specific service a week, which would reduce the time, demanded of each team member.

Just a quick note: Many team members who started serving a designated service have eventually expanded their coverage and many will be present at 2 or 3 services a week. God has blessed us with many fine Christ-like servants. Now we worry more about running out of radios and ear pieces – which is not a bad problem to have.

Adopting the SOGs, our goal became to fill each of nine positions, for four services at our church, and to also establish the same team structure at two other campuses who each have 2 Sunday services, for a total of 8 teams or 72 volunteers in our ministry. It seems like a very lofty goal, but cutting time requirements to one service per week and one training event per month should make committing to the security ministry easier for a lot of people.

Additional benefits of increasing ministry size is greater security presence which will provide a greater deterrence, increased ability to detect threats and react to them with enough backup to help keep our team and people close to the incident safer. More team members responding also increases potential for delaying threats or disrupters with better de-escalation success. And it provides a reliable schedule to the church and gives team members more options to ask others to fill in if they can't attend their scheduled service.

Defining roles is important. Right now, we are recruiting for 4 groups within our ministry: worship security, EMS, team leaders, and personal pastoral security. Each team member has different responsibilities. For example, EMS needs to possess a current certification of EMT or above. They are expected to maintain this certification through their work or other volunteer activities. Definitions can also be altered to fit team needs.

Consult with pastors, directors, and any relevant committees, employees and existing volunteers. You may want to consider the following questions. What is the function of volunteers and what tasks are volunteers suited to? What skills and experience would the organization want volunteers to bring to their position?

How will the organization go about finding volunteers? What will the selection process involve? If volunteers are successfully recruited, how will the organization ensure they remain with the organization? Examine your retention practices and make sure your ministry has something to offer volunteers in the way of fulfillment.

As we are led by the Holy Spirit, we understand that at any time, the Holy Spirit could lead us in a totally different direction. Team members are reminded to support each other in our prodding's. Our goal is to serve as part of the body and we have to recognize that when we make this about us, we could be pushing someone to change churches.

Rather than push to have anyone serve only with our team, we must encourage others to explore other areas of service at the church. Above all, we need to create a home where everyone is comfortable.

Now, it's time to get out the word. Advertising for new volunteers requires an organization to prepare its message to potential volunteers and choose channels for recruitment. For example, we will make an appeal to our men's ministry. The key here is to be persistent and be patient. The team will grow as more people are added.

Recently, I was approached by our Chaplin Training Director who told me she and her husband have changed their volunteer requirement to include mainly volunteering at our church. When she explained this to me, I said, "Great! When do you want me to come in and give a presentation?"

I can almost guarantee she's never had one person say this.

When I started on our team, we were just wearing street clothes. Ushers, greeters, staff, and volunteers were aware that a team existed, but the reality was that if you didn't see our radio earpiece and you didn't know who we were, you probably were suspicious of who it was exactly that was lurking in the church.

Initially, a veteran usher noticed my wife Kathy and I as new attendees. He greeted us, welcomed us, made us feel at home and suggested we could get involved with the church. So, I asked about joining a security team. To which he said, "I don't know…but I'll find out for you."

An opportunity existed to create a way the volunteer security team was identifiable. Now, everyone knows. And, everyone feels natural approaching us. They know where to direct others with questions and concerns.

If your team is small, this isn't as much of a concern as it would be when church membership increases. Mainly, it is the constant addition and subtraction of volunteers that obliges us to provide some sort of identification. Ushers are apparent, but when people need to turn to someone for a security or EMS reason, they need a way to know who is who.

Currently, our ushers and greeters wear an identifier on a lanyard. It lets everyone know they are ushers. Problem is, these identifiers are left lying around and basically anyone can take one. Thinking like a criminal, I could see getting ahold of one these lanyards and standing up to collect the offerings. Who would object to the new person volunteering? Certainly, we don't want anyone getting a security ID and pretending to be security.

We developed a simple, cost efficient method of identification that we'll go into greater detail on. But, once we began identifying ourselves, the team size doubled in just two months. People who asked about the identifier found that we had a team. Most people never knew this. And a few asked if they could join us.

Likewise, as we expanded to our second campus, the team leader there was wondering how they would build the team. I suggested just wearing the team identifier and the very next week the team doubled in size.

Actively recruiting is ongoing – there is never a time to give up on recruiting. It is an ongoing process of finding the best-qualified candidates from within your organization to fill positions in a ministry geared to protect others. There is no financial compensation for working during services or attending training. The recruitment process includes analyzing the requirements of the position, attracting congregants to that position, screening and selecting applicants, training them and integrating the new volunteer into the team.

Applicants may be eager to serve, but they may not qualify based upon SOG requirements. For example, our SOGs suggest a candidate must have been a member of the church for six months to be on the security team. An interested person may have only been at the church for a month, like I was. And then, there are gray areas – we just accepted a new team member who had been a church member, left a few years ago, and just came back. While he was away, he acquired some negative smudges on his record. Gray areas are instances where conditions could exclude the applicant from team participation, but extenuating circumstances, if considered, may present a unique opportunity.

Background checks are an integral part of the team membership process.

Every security member is required to complete and pass a background check upon applying for the position and at least once every three years. Forgiveness and grace, not judging others has worked very well for me in my life, but so has discernment. I believe most people, me included, have room for improvement. Developing team members is best achieved with a written plan for everyone to follow. It takes prejudice and the "good-old-boy" club syndrome out of the equation and allows everyone to have an equal opportunity.

After reviewing an application and conducting an interview a recommendation is made and forwarded to pastors for consideration. I enjoy talking to applicants about their background check results, their personal goals, opportunities offered through our church, and a vision that includes them. In the end, clear communications that include purpose, scope, goals, SOGs, and expectations provides a very smooth and predictable result that will be fulfilling to the team member; allow them to see where their gifts can positively affect church mission, vision, and goals. Ministry should always provide the experience of fulfillment and allow volunteers to utilize their God given gifts.

We do have a process where negative background checks can be overridden. For example, I approached an usher who had said he was interested in getting involved with the security team, but indicated he had quite a record and doubted he would ever be able to serve in that capacity. He came to Jesus more than two decades ago, has served as an usher faithfully for many years, and is a very caring empathetic person. Two security leaders and the ministry's pastor agreed that he should be able to serve on the security team. I wish I could show you a picture of the look on his face when we told him he was confirmed. Priceless! I have no doubt that he will serve the team well. He has been very dependable and adds to the value and culture of our team.

Another applicant was in prison more recently, but not for a crime that would exclude him from the team. He's getting his life back together, has a Christ-like heart, and is committed to our church and our team.

A few years ago this person was basically homeless and his future was unclear. He was told to come to the church for food and shelter. When he walked into the church he was greeted by man who asked if he needed anything. Without hesitation, the man reached into his pocket and gave this guy some money to get something to eat.

This single act of kindness, from a total stranger, caused this team member to "Let go and let God." He atoned for his sins, paid his debt to society, and received God's mercy and grace. His compassion, understanding, and desire to serve this ministry is outstanding.

Fast forward a couple years after our new team member reaffirmed Christ in his life and got things turned around. Prior to the fragmented times of his life, and before our team structure was in place, he did serve on our churches security team. Upon his return, he sought to once again serve in the capacity of worship security.

Now this person leads a group of men at his workplace. He works five or six twelve hour shifts a week. And most important, he's getting his life together. When I was introduced to him, he told me about the guy at our church who gave him the twenty dollars that changed his life a few years earlier. In fact, the event was so impactful on his life that he repeated the story again to me the next week. And then I was blessed to witness a great reunion. As God events tend to turn out, the person who gave him the money was also currently active on our security team.

New guy looked at veteran guy and said, "You don't remember me do you?" Veteran guy couldn't imagine where he would ever have met this person. New guy told him the story…talked about how that act helped him get his life back together and said it was an act of kindness he will never forget.

Veteran guy replies without missing a beat. He said that his wife had just passed away when they met the first time. He had just attended a sermon where the pastor was talking about the importance of giving. This act of kindness was a healing for him too.

In certain circumstances, overriding negative background checks may benefit the team. There are some issues where we do draw a line such as any sexual predator type of offense. Our stand is that anyone listed on the sexual predator list should find a ministry where they do not have access to others who may be more vulnerable, especially children.

We have a few missing children alerts every year. Thank God, all have been found and reunited with their parents. Imagine the scenario of having a missing child alert and your first thought is, where is this person on your team who has been charged the pedophile crime?

Expanding our team's volunteer numbers created 9 additional leadership positions. It's been a year and all 9 of those positions have been filled. Just a reminder, teams like this do not come together over night.

Team leaders, along with our pastor, meet once per month to discuss worship security ministry topics, including questions about applications, background checks, and other issues. We seek majority agreement to handle sensitive issues like failed checks or applicants who do not meet current guidelines for team membership.

A pastor referred someone to our team that was an Afghanistan war veteran. Though he had been attending our church, he felt he could recruit the help of some of his war buddies who also suffered from PTSD. Our goal was to protect the integrity of the team, but we did create a system of people who wanted to be mentors, that would serve with the war veterans.

I'm sorry to report that at this time, no one has taken the offer. But we were prepared for it.

A couple weeks ago, a veteran who fought in Panama joined us. He too has PTSD. We had an EMS call for a woman who broke her wrist. The look on face afterward, being able to help someone in need, told me he'll be around for a long while. Through this team, I pray that he finds what he is looking for. There's a lot of support among the team for his success.

Our goal of attaining enough team members to have each person serve at only one specified service a week really means recruiting a team of 74 security and 9 EMS team members. Though we started with just 6 team members serving 3 services, we are now at almost 50 team members (including EMS) serving 9 services. It does take effort, but once the effort is made, it is a team responsibility.

Several of our team members have brought candidates to our attention.

Our pastors and staff members are now recommending people to our ministry.

Our focus now is recruiting about a dozen more security people, 6 more certified EMS, and we are developing team leaders. Every service now has a Team Leader and an Assistant Team Leader. One day someone will take over for me and it's important to me that this person has been trained I every aspect.

For parody's sake, let's face it....Jesus might have said, where two or more are gathered...there's going to be politics.

Starting or improving a security/EMS team is often a very political debate in church. I don't want my Assistant Team Director, or any of our leaders to have to go through what our team has already gone through politically. To avoid this, I include them in every aspect of our team growth, development, and the issues that come up from time –to-time.

Eventually, we like to continue to grow the team to be able to provide security to other ministries. Hence, recruiting is ongoing. Be patient, but be persistent. Continually encourage current team members to promote and recruit for the team. Having a membership section in your SOGs will explain the process and make recruiting easier.

Ranking worship service risks and requirements allowed us to focus on which services would provide the greatest opportunity to implement the new changes. Starting out by training our existing team the new SOGs over a three month period gave us a luxury of exposing the team to change where we could demonstrate positive results and get individuals to buy in to the new processes. During training, we also continually reiterate that the SOGs are just a start and that they can be changed to reflect church needs, changes in "best practices," and variations designed for each campus to better serve their members. In any case, change should be the expectation.

Originally, it was felt that our SOGs should be printed by the church, on church letterhead, and bound. But, we have found that constantly changing information requires us to edit the SOGs once in a while. For that reason, our SOGs are basically in a Word format, making it easier to make changes and resend the new guidelines.

Communicating change(s) is always important. The concept of one team per service was shared in a weekly email that. Even the email communication process was new as we had begun employing it just two weeks earlier – another change incorporated. One week after the "new" goal was shared, our first two team leaders were established, team members picked service times they would be accountable for, and another change was embraced.

There is a caveat to the new procedure. At this point we still haven't reached our goal 72 team members; as of the original writing of this book, we weren't even at the halfway point. Current team members have been asked to pick a service they will eventually have as their main service once teams are staffed correctly and they have been asked to also continue current practices of volunteering at multiple services.

All new team members are assigned a mentor for at least a month. By the end of the month, or before, we'll know if this person fits into the position or not. At our monthly team training, the new team member is introduced and the mentor can speak freely about their experience to date with the new applicant. Upon approval, the new team member is added to a permanent crew.

Team size
According to Wikipedia, "A megachurch is an American term for a church having 2,000 or more people in average weekend attendance. In 2010, the Hartford Institute's database listed more than 1,300 such Protestant churches in the United States; according to that data, approximately 50 churches on the list had average monthly attendance exceeding 10,000, with the highest recorded at 47,000 in average attendance.

On one weekend in November 2015, around one in ten Protestant churchgoers in the US, or about 5 million people, attended service in a megachurch. While 3,000 individual Catholic parishes (churches) have 2,000 or more attendants for an average Sunday Mass, these churches are not seen as part of the megachurch movement. In the United States, the phenomenon has more than quadrupled in the past two decades. It has since spread worldwide.

As of this writing, the largest megachurch in the United States is Lakewood Church in Houston, Texas with more than 40,000 members every weekend and the current largest megachurch in the world is South Korea's Yoido Full Gospel Church, an Assemblies of God church, with more than 830,000 members as of 2007."

Lakewood Church meets in a former sports arena with seating for 16,000. The origins of the megachurch movement, with a large number of local congregants who return on a weekly basis can be traced to the 1950s.

The size of your church, risks identified in the risk assessment, number of services held, campus size, other activities, parking, scope of team responsibilities, etc. are all considerations for team size. Only 3.5% of churches in the US are mega churches.

If you're like the majority of US churches, 59% have less than 99 congregants attending weekly services (excluding Catholic Church). 35% have weekly attendance below 500. Yet, possibly the most important statistic is that almost 99% of U.S. churches do not have a formal policy or any guidelines for their security team; regardless of whether or not their team is an actual team recognized by the church, or just a congregant who assumes the position. And, all these churches may be open to acts of violence and/or liability claims that could potentially ruin them.

Starting with leadership, an effective span of control is between seven and twelve reports. Span of control refers to the number of people who reports to a leader. Fortune 500 CEOs report the average number of direct reports is 7.44. A direct report is anyone under the leader who follows their instruction. Reports are accountable to team leaders and team leaders are accountable to pastors who are accountable to the church.

Creating the right team dynamics is paramount in determining success or failure of the team. Any leader's ability (or lack thereof) to effectively attract, train, deploy and retain volunteer team members will tell you everything you need to know about said leader. We've all been on teams that succeed and others that don't meet expectations. Smart leaders seek to be challenged and to encourage diversity of thought and dissenting opinion. One of the primary drivers of team composition should be to find a group of talented individuals who will challenge, stretch, and develop leadership and the team.

How far a team can be stretched, is not the question or the goal. We are volunteers, not workers on an assembly line. It's not about getting teams to produce more with less resources, it is about succeeding in our goals to protect the church, which also must consider protecting the team.

Leaders must be accountable to their people or they will eventually be held accountable by their people. One of a leader's most important functions is to create an environment where trust and loyalty are the rule and not the exception. This is especially true if our core missions, visions, and goals are to be achieved.

Risk assessments and service coverage are the first determining factors of team size. If your church is smaller than 100 people, you're in a community where everyone knows each other, you're holding one or two services a week, your pastor is not controversial, there are only a couple of entrances, etc., you may only need 3 people on your team.

On the other hand, if you a congregation of 400, with two services on Sunday and another on Wednesday, you're in a high crime area, and have multiple entrances, you will want a larger team. More on this discussion to come!

Assignments will also be defined by your "Scope." Who, what, where, and when you are protecting and for how long?

In our "Scope" we define the "who," starting with the Executive Pastor and then extending to staff, volunteers, and the congregation. Our "what," are the risks we assessed at our church. For us, our "Where," is in the church building as a different volunteer group is assigned to the outside perimeter, just as personal protection is assigned different duties. Our SOGs apply only to the volunteer teem inside the building. And, "when," is during services.

Church size is not really as relevant. Congregant attendance on Wednesday may be as many as 20 people. In this case adding 10 people to attendance would be big. Sunday at our church ranges from a low of 600 at the first service to a high of 3,000 in the second service. The same team of 9 can effectively work with most church sizes. More relevant would be the risk assessment and what the team scope and goals are. You may find you have 3 main doors people enter from and decide you want those doors covered at every service. If that takes 3 team members out of the position assignments for the worship service, you may need twelve team members to achieve your goals.

Important to remember, we cannot stop everyone who wants to disrupt or harm others. We cannot prevent all destruction and theft from every aspect of our church's property. We can only be expected to provide and inspire the most excellent service we can, implement a plan that works almost all of the time, and train, train, train.

We have 4 main doors on 2 levels that people use to enter and exit our facility. Only two of the doors are our "main" entrance, so it gets more attention. We used to place team members behind the stage, but on our campus and historically, while the potential of an attack or disturbance from the backstage area is a possibility, it is much more likely that any attack or disturbance that might happen will come from our audience in front of the podium. Since our resources are limited, we need to focus our attention on the higher risk areas.

The larger the church campus and the greater the scope of security needs, the more team members it will take to staff. Our volunteer security team currently only provides security during church services. There are also uniformed security guards on campus 24/7 who are also responsible for responding to the children's classes in a separate building, there is a parking lot ministry that keeps an eye on the parking lots, and there are pastors who assume other security roles.

Fill assignments based on scope, but try not to judge or become overly focused on an area that you feel may be vulnerable in the security perimeter. Take a 360 degree view and always consider the need to provide backup for team members.

In the fire service, a team leader who gets hyper focused on one concern is missing the action occurring all around them. This is called tunnel vision; "A defective sight in which objects cannot be properly seen if not close to the center of the field of view." "The tendency to focus exclusively on a single or limited goal or point of view," – according to google. Tunnel vision detracts from our ability to fully be aware of our surroundings, thus reducing situational awareness.

Utilizing the same team members we had before, but placing the two that were behind the stage in front of the stage gave our team an increase in presence and awareness, which can deter people from creating disturbances. It also gave us more options in response and increased safety among individuals on our team.

Setting some sort of guideline of "X" Staff per "X" congregants doesn't usually work. Nightclubs may ascribe to the 1:35 or 1:50 security to patron ratio, depending upon the type of crowd. A theme park may use 1:1,000. Our scope is limited to the church, during services and our main function is to protect the pastor(s). So, we determine advantageous positions, based upon our belief that threats will usually take the path of least resistance. Typically, they are not going to plan an elaborate scheme to achieve their goals as the primary driver is anger. This is also why creating deterrents, like identifiable security, can discourage a threat who is considering some type of action and why de-escalation training is so important.

Our exposures, and most churches will have this in common, is the stage area and the aisles leading to it. We have 4 very long aisles leading from the back of the auditorium, where our main entry doors are, that go all the way to the stage. So, we place at least one security person at the stage end of each aisle. There are also provisions for the personal protection of the pastor. We have positions at main entrances, roamers, and EMS.

This is an optimal set up. Later on I will detail the positions and list them in order of importance. Assignments start with position #1 located on the left side of the stage and move in a clockwise manner. With this predictable set up, every team member from any campus can replace another security person if needed, or volunteer on a different campus, and everyone is on the same page.

Some churches may be able to operate with fewer teams. I find volunteers like the balance of at least two teams; one can be on duty while the other gets to sit in on the service. Sunday morning, team "A" would take the

9:00 am service and team "B" the 11:00 am service. If your church desires to do this, you may have 18 positions that need to be filled.

Most important to the security of the church and the safety and efficiency of the team is to plan where two to three team members have the ability to respond to an interruption without pulling team members assigned to the front of the stage away from their positions. During services, team members do not close their eyes or bow their heads and should continually be scanning the audience to try and detect unwanted behavior before it happens.

Alone, one team member may not be able to quiet a disturbance or de-escalate a threat. However, a show of force through additional backup may help de-escalate the situation just by presenting an abundance of team. An angry person may lash out violently with one person, but may decide it is an unwinnable situation with three team members there. This also can resolve conflicts sooner, allowing security to return to their assigned posts, making them more efficient.

Strategic planning is a systematic process of envisioning a desired future or longer term result. It creates a foundation based on broadly defined goals or objectives and a sequence of steps to achieve them. This purposeful process allows us to act independently, while at the same time assuring our activity and actions help the church achieve its goals.

Problems are opportunities for improvement. Every stage of planning allows us to ask, "What must be done here to reach the next (higher) level?" Working towards excellence begs us to ask, "What must be done at the previous (lower) level to take us to become the team we envision?" What better praise can we offer God than excellence in our acts?

If we took the time to compare police, fire, emergency medical, and other emergency response – we would find an increasing competence and professionalism designed to add value to the community, offer greater protection and probability of survival for the community and the rescue teams serving them, all while attempting to reduce liability. I believe we owe it to our congregation and our churches to assume similar views regarding our worship security teams.

Our churches are undergoing a massive transformation as they respond to changing social needs of our modern society. Just as changes occur in every field, churches must modify their processes to attract, retain, and ensure the safety of their congregants. Changes in firefighting tactics and control offer a great example of the evolution from a heart driven organization to a one that retains the heart, but offers more analytical and technical applications to help save lives.

Firefighting strategies for fighting fires have become more technical since the late 1960's. Self-contained breathing apparatus (SCBA) was just being put into use. This allowed firefighters the ability to enter buildings and breathe in an otherwise toxic environment. It was both a safety and rescue improvement.

But, SCBA had its limits. An air bottle only lasted about 20 minutes, based on how heavy the person wearing the tank was breathing. An out of shape smoker could suck up a bottle of in just 14 minutes. When air supply gets low alarms start to off and teams were pulled out of the fight early. Learning to deal with this was a part of the transformation.

About that same time, new chemicals, artificial fabrics, and plastics became prevalent in building materials, furnishings, clothing, etc. Old construction, furniture, etc. became known as a "legacy" fire. New homes are now referred to as modern fires and the average heat produced has gone from about 700 degrees to over 1,600 degrees. It only takes 700 degrees to melt steel.

Throw in new roof truss construction, weatherization processes, and other factors and fires today act much differently than they did before the late 1960s. Unfortunately, this also meant more danger to firefighters.

An even bigger problem was fire-ground command when a firefighter was down in a burning building. Every firefighter is assigned a position. There is a first line in, a second line backup, an engineer (1 per truck). There may be water-flow operations, EMS staging, roof ventilation, search and rescue operations, water curtain use protecting exposures from radiant heat, aerial tower and ladder teams, staging officers, command, and other functions all going on at the same time. The success of the operation is dependent upon everyone doing their job – just like our security teams.

Problems occurred when a firefighter went down. Other firefighters left their positions to help their downed or possibly trapped brothers and sisters. Fires not being suppressed got larger and compromised building integrity that could threaten responders, eliminated escape routes, and sometimes meant the death of those responding.

Responding to this new challenge, fire departments began assembling rapid intervention teams, sometimes referred to as RIT, FAST, or Technical Rescue teams. Their job is solely to respond to firefighters in trouble, with the goal being to assure everyone else stays in their assigned positions.

Our churches are going through transformations as well. The obvious security concerns of higher violence, higher poverty and unemployment, more drug abuse, desensitized youth who play violent video games, a move by secular America to remove God from the community, internet, child pornography, and so much more. My parent's places of worship never had to deal with this. And it's coming faster and faster than ever before.

Security teams need the same considerations, which is why we stress the importance of deterring potential disrupters and backing up team members who detect people who may not have been deterred. More details will be provided later in the book when assignments are discussed.

I also was certified to train FEMA "Response to Terrorism" classes to fire departments. Criminals, terrorists, and people threatening violence may test your system to see response protocols to find holes in security. If an incident occurs on the left side of the sanctuary that pulls security from the front and right sides, it may give them the opportunity they seek.

Team size should be determined by need, scope, and goals of the ministry. Make sure to identify all needs through a risk analysis and recruit enough volunteers that allow you to achieve those goals.

Finally, not every applicant will be appropriate for your team for one reason or another. It may be someone who served time for a sexual offense. It could be the wanna-be cop who sees this as an opportunity to prove themselves. Whatever the reason, the SOGs can provide a solid reason for denying team membership ONLY if SOG standards are applied equally to every candidate. Applying principles to each candidate without discrimination can lower the potential for a discrimination claim.

Chapter 4

TRAINING

During my service as a volunteer firefighter, I was blessed to meet and train with like-minded individuals. Not everyone in our fire department held the same values, urgency, or drive and for some it was very obvious by their performance. We trained constantly and helped teach our department's firefighters what we learned. Yes, we understood that we may have been the anomaly when it comes to volunteers; we were certainly not the norm. Leadership set the bar, and it was continually reset it based on our training, education, and research.

I would be remiss if I didn't mention the desire of others in our field to reach out – especially when they recognized a team that wanted to step up its performance. Ron Naab, a very humble servant of God, and a volunteer firefighter (Chief-Retired) himself, has done more than anyone I'm aware of to bring quality training to thousands of firefighters in multiple states around Wisconsin.

When I was asked to come aboard a nonprofit group called, "Specialist

Code III." Ron was running it. He surrounded himself with some of the most amazing people. I was honored to serve among them. These firefighters became mentors and inspired me to always seek more education. But most important was their desire to share, to help improve others. And, they did it for free.

Likewise, when it comes to church security we have caring people like Carl Chin from Colorado, and Mark Fritts who is a security director at church near me. He also leads a group of church security directors from Mesa, Gilbert, and Chandler, AZ and brings them together once a month to discuss the latest and greatest, share opportunities, and hold a roundtable discussion regarding issues church security teams may be facing. I would guess that there about 30 churches participating. Again, it's an honor to be somewhat associated with servants like this.

We never know what God has in store for us. This includes His plans for us to prosper. In Charismamagazine 06/29/2015, Mike Shreve wrote: "6 Earmarks of a Modern-Day Esther." Reflecting on the last line of (Esth. 4:14) – "And who knows if you may have attained royal position for such a time as this?"

Mr. Shreve lists six behaviors he felt were important in describing Esther and comparing her achievement, saving an entire group of people who were threatened with annihilation.

He lists "Virtue" as the number one characteristic and says, "...those who will be used mightily of God in this hour must hold virtue, integrity and holiness in high esteem—walking the walk, not just talking the talk.

Second, "Esther had a mentor." "And so the prophets and prophetesses of this hour can point to the previous generation of men and women of God who held the torch high for us."

Next is that, "Esther was willing to leave her comfort zone." He adds, "...or we can step out of our comfort zones to help an endangered world and to advance the cause of the kingdom of God."

Mike reminds us, "Remember the acronym for TEAM—Together Everyone Accomplishes More." And he lists, "Esther's ability to mobilize others." He cites Esther's willingness to accept risk and writes, "God is searching the world over for those who are willing to risk it all in order to fulfill God's purposes, thwart enemy plans and see their full potential awakened."

Finally, and most important, Shreve writes, "Esther was part of a plan." And he includes, "The Bible says that God has "saved us and called us with a holy calling, not by our works, but by His own purpose and grace, which was given us in Christ Jesus before the world began" (2 Tim. 1:9).

Mike ends by writing, "Do your part. Step into your destiny."

You have a servant's heart. You focus on living a Christ driven life. You find the Holy Spirit providing purpose and calling in being the shepherd - watching over the flock. Then you may be in the right ministry. Learning the most efficient way to be of service to your church is to accept changes and be willing to learn - which is a byproduct of training.

After completing the basic firefighting requirements for the state of Wisconsin, I was offered an opportunity to attend a "Farm Rescue" class near Steven's Point, WI. This is where I first met Ron Naab and his Code III crew. Certainly, other communities had a bigger call for farm rescue training than mine.

My community had plenty of farms, but most were hobby farms and most of our thirty six square mile coverage area was new building construction. However, the training was cutting edge and I found that people who are passionate about their service like to be the best at what they do.

Conveniently, at the time I had attended the Code III event, was in the midst of a job change. I was selling advertising for Milwaukee's oldest and largest rock-n-roll radio station. It just wasn't satisfying; The Holy Spirit pushed me toward serving the community and helping people in need. I started reading fire department trade magazines and saw an article on hazardous materials (haz-mat) response. The year was 1991 and haz-mat was fairly new. Most fire departments had no real SOGs on hazardous materials response.

There were several classes' firefighters and EMS could choose from in this two day farm rescue class by Code III. My love was in extrication and they had a few seminars dedicated to heavy machinery rescue, including removing patients from corn pickers and hay bailers. All very interesting and more technical, but it was the one mandatory class – "Anhydrous Ammonia and You," that I objected to. I never signed up for it and it was two hours long! What could anyone possibly have to say about this stuff that would take two hours?

At this point, I made myself a deal. I thought, if I could make it through this class with my eyeballs still intact, I was going to explore a career in hazardous materials response.

Screaming and kicking in my mind, imagining that I could fall asleep if I wanted to, I walked to the dreaded class. I remember they served us coffee and soft drinks, cookies, cake, and other good treats. If memory serves me right, I believe I made some wise comment about how they needed to sugar us up so we didn't fall asleep.

Exactly to the minute of the scheduled start, some guy from Cenex – a supplier of anhydrous ammonia to farmers and industry – walked to the middle of the stage, looked out at the group and proclaimed, "Anhydrous Ammonia boils at 27 degrees below zero."

I was hooked. I never knew anything boiled at temperatures below zero. As for the rest of the training – it was amazing! To this day, I can recite that this chemical is heavier than air, meaning the plume of vapor (vapor results from boiling liquid) will stay closer to the ground. It expands at a ratio of three hundred to one, meaning a one inch leak of liquid will expand to three hundred square inches of vapor.

Upon return from the class, I immediately went to interview several haz-mat firefighters in Milwaukee. At the time, there was only a forty hour Occupational Safety Health Administration (OSHA) training program and a two year degreed program from Lakeshore Technical College in Cleveland WI. I was advised to take the two year course.

As the Holy Spirit works…because I attended a training session, one that I particularly didn't want to attend, I chose a new career and switched from advertising sales to haz-mat response. I was hired by an independent contractor to manage his haz-mat response team, but he soon developed business problems and I found myself starting a company that pulled underground storage tanks and cleaned contaminated soil.

Full circle: Code III is a nonprofit organization that teaches firefighters and EMS technical rescue techniques. They put on the symposium on farm rescue. A few years later I would be blessed to be a part of their training team.

Training is an opportunity to make and correct mistakes that don't cost anything. Worship security teams may never come in contact with our worst case scenarios, but it's reassuring to feel prepared for anything. Attending one training session doesn't make someone proficient, but continual consistent training can. Developing a training program is simple, when SOGs are in place.

For many church security teams, training is a tough mountain to climb. But imagine if your worship team didn't practice – would you really look forward to hearing them as they miss notes and fumble to remember lyrics? What if the children's ministry never met? You get the point…teams have to train together to be effective.

I've included personal stories in this book to help demonstrate that having procedures is necessary and training is imperative. But if any reader here were to look in their past and examine opportunities for excellence, times when things didn't always go according to plan, including times when everything wrong and the cost may have been higher than normal, you would find similar stories. The goal must be to give our security teams every possible advantage as we strive for excellence.

Below is a copy of our training SOG, followed by a training agenda we use for our monthly training. Notice how all the training refers to a current SOG. That's it. Know your SOGs, decide what's important to teach or identify an area of opportunity for improvement and put it on the training schedule. The schedule is flexible, allows team leaders to observe team operations and target training to areas of need, creating the opportunity for improved performance.

As I'm writing this book, which will end up being about a two year long project, I'm including real stories about conversations and events from my church and our team. I'm starting at the beginning and bringing up examples of where we started, obstacles we faced, and vision for where we are going.

Also, as I'm writing, our team is still growing. Over the now 24 months, since I started writing a lot has happened. Rather than delete past events written about, I believe this is a good opportunity to demonstrate conflicts that may occur and supply those of you passionate enough, with tools to move your team further. While persistence and follow through may work with some of your team members who are not on board with changes, sometimes the answer can be found in reading how others have overcome similar issues.

Here's an original story: One of my favored team members was also a bit of a mentor to me. He showed me around on the first day I began serving on the security team and he has been a great sounding board for me. As our team began this journey of change, before anything was written out, before anyone embraced the new guidelines, he was my go-to-guy for questions and insight. He got copies of many things during the planning stages including drafts of the new SOGs, all seeking his input.

One day, we were alone on the 3rd floor balcony. I asked him why he never replied to any of the rough draft SOGs I had sent him. He got a bit loud and seemed kind of angry that the "powers that be" wouldn't allow this team growth to happen. Certainly in that moment, he was right, I just didn't want to hear it.

Although his response was not the optimistic conversation I had hoped for, I did appreciate the input. When people around me are negative, I am thankful for the diversity and imagine it is more of an anchor that God may be sending to keep me from moving too fast in a direction that others may be hesitant to follow. I respect his opinion and his advice – as always.

From my point of view: Starting with the identification pin that I felt was a team unifier and identifier necessary to help us achieve our first goal of deterring, he didn't feel the need to wear it. He worked on Saturdays and was never able to attend training. And fairly soon after communications started, he kind of distanced himself from the team, which broke my heart. I was counting on this person to be a leader, but quickly realized that leaders need to buy into the program. He was recommended as a team trainer by a pastor, which would have been an amazing opportunity. My attitude was that we can't have someone teach what they won't practice.

Over the course of a few months, I tried to figure out ways to get my friend more active with the team. It was hard, because giving in to him would mean compromising the entire program. In my head, the questions kept repeating: What if someone else on the team decides not wear a pin or not to follow protocol. Worse yet, we were in the starting stages of organizing – what if someone quit?

Well, I'm glad to share that yes, several people wouldn't wear pins. Yes, several people didn't want to follow protocol, and yes several people quit. There! I worried for nothing.

Still, over time, even our small discussions became short and more pointed. Eventually, we stopped talking to each other all together. That was real rough.

In due course, I created a position I had imagined he would love and asked if he'd be interested. His answer was, "I don't know if I can do that, I'm kind of a free bird."

I have great respect for this man; I prayed that he would find fulfillment in this ministry, or find the strength to move to a ministry where his gifts would help escalate that group and unfortunately my writings most likely created the impression that I would rather have him leave.

I felt my first responsibility was to the church and those on the team that have committed to being shepherds and I didn't allow myself to understand his point of view. I allowed his "Free bird" statement to stay in my mind and had an attitude of, "We don't have free birds on our team – it's not fair to the team." I take responsibility for my role in this conflict, as a leader, friend, and brother in Christ.

The new addition to that story: I prayed many times for God to show me wisdom in this situation as I believe this teammate too was praying for direction. Sometimes, when God doesn't answer right away it just means we have to give the condition more time. After three months of not talking to each other, I was discussing the situation with Phoenix Police Officer Mark, an off duty uniformed police department officer who works at our church during services and special events. He took me into stairwell and we began praying for guidance.

It wasn't 5 minutes later that a pastor approached me and told me about a meeting he had just had with this team member. Everything was a complete misunderstanding. Next service, this person showed up, put on a radio, took an assignment and signed into the security log. He is an amazing asset to our team and I am grateful for his participation. We are blessed to have him serve with us.

I learned that most of our troubles may have stemmed from my email communications. In our email system, everyone on the team is bulk emailed, but only the receiver's name appears in the header. This person worked when we had training and thought the emails were specifically being sent to him and no one else. I know I very well might feel the same way. What a shame it would have been to lose this person who I consider a wonderful asset over something as simple as this.

Managing a team means managing through change. As the old adage goes, nothing is certain but change. Most people do not take change well. As we get older, it seems even the slightest changes tend to throw us off. Hence, delicate situations will occur. Later, we talk about "Leadership." Suffice for now to say, team leaders succeed when they lead by example. Be the change you need to see.

Assuming every person from the old team is going to enthusiastically accept new changes can cost volunteer team members. As managers, we often are faced with employees who do not buy into our system and we are encouraged by upper management to let these people go, sometimes very quickly. But this is not a paid position. We count on volunteers to fill our teams and protect our church as threat assessors and first responders. Having a heavy hand may reduce team size and ability, and may hamper new volunteer recruitment. Just think about the politics and rumor mill at your church – it's probably faster than the newest technology for the internet.

Approach each individual with a Christ-like heart. Have patience and allow the team to develop. In the end, a little understanding may go a long way. Follow the Holy Spirit and allow God's will to seep in. Explain this with mercy, grace, and forgiveness to your team. Pray for direction, instruction, and guidance.

The larger your team, the more diverse your team members will be. Be prepared with your heart and mind. Change does take time, but it will come – just keep shooting for excellence. Training puts everyone on the same page, or at least attempts to. It helps new team members understand your team's processes and allows the team to buy into your vision. .

Training SOG:

2.1 Training
Basic training on topics deemed important by the VST will be conducted and attendance documented. A training file for each member will be started and updated as new training is conducted. Training is the most important part of our VST program. On-going training will serve to increase interest and protect our church from changing threats and legal issues that often arise when no training or inadequate training occurs.

1. Training will occur one (1) time per month on the second Saturday of each month or as per VST Director.

2. One day per year will be dedicated to a mandatory all-day training.

3. Additional training sessions may be called by team leaders and/or may require time changes to accommodate outside instructors and guest speakers.

4. Training may include lecture style, class participation, practice drills, reading, internet research, and other methods of instruction.

5. All team members will be notified in advance of meeting dates and location.

6. Safety team members are expected to make at least (8) eight of (11) eleven training sessions annually.

7. EMS team members must attend mandatory VST training, but are exempt from 2.1 (6) training requirements. EMS leader will determine any training for EMS volunteers.

Training should be conducted on a specific unmovable date, time, and location. Team members need to be able to plan around training, which they can only do if they know when training will occur, where it will be held, and what time they need make allowance for. It is up to team leaders and trainers to assure that training occurs when it is scheduled to take place.

Certainly it would be easier on the leaders and trainers if the times and places could be more flexible. But leading is never about the leader – it is about the people they lead – especially in this case where we are all volunteers. So, an annual training calendar is created and adhered to. Our training is held on the second Saturday of the month at our main campus at 10:00am. Just make sure your training does not occur on a holiday or holiday weekend.

We have begun a Team leader meeting that starts an hour earlier than the monthly training. Everyone is invited, allowing team members to hear what team leaders are talking about.

Monthly training utilizes a set agenda to assure all points of a meeting are covered. Section one is a formal agenda. Items on the agenda have been included to assure each topic is covered. We can skip topics that don't need to be covered.

For example, we have training attendees sign in on a sign in sheet that we will keep with training outline and filed away monthly by year. This allows us to provide evidence of training, along with the training outline to insurance auditors and in cases where one of our team members may be called into question or have liability issues against them or the church. In our Blood Bourne Pathogen training, we train team members to wear gloves when bodily fluids may potentially be encountered in a response. If a team member was exposed, and didn't follow precautions, and then sued the church, we could provide training documentation that were correctly instructed.

We do train our team basic bleeding control techniques that necessarily does require responders to wear gloves and where they are located.

Training session attendees also take a name tag. We really don't need to have a roll call, because we do have a sign in sheet. Rather than eliminate the item from the agenda, it is kept there just in case someone else takes over training. It also helps keep us on track timewise.

Section two is classroom or chalkboard, where we will discuss the SOGs and answer questions related to Section three – practical training. Keep in mind that people learn in different ways. Some people are audio learners and have to hear what is being taught. Some are visual learners and need to see the process on paper, a white board, or slide show. And others learn by doing, which is one reason we have the practical application training.

Time estimates are included in each of the three main categories to assure trainers comply with time expectations. Certainly there are instances where timing will be longer or shorter than planned and in some cases where the trainer feels one area, like practical training needs to be longer, they can adjust other times down and increase time where they want to spend more time.

Critical incident stress will be discussed further in this book, but after a stressful incident, team members may want to spend more time talking about the incident. I would encourage trainers to follow the needs flow, but to also remember that people who learn by doing will have more questions during the audio or visual presentation. If you feel time is being wasted by redundant questions or that some team members require more information, a good tactic is to go through the process and take questions after the practical exercises.

Below is an agenda for our monthly team training:

Worship Security Monthly Meeting/Training Outline

Date: _____

Section 1: Worship Security Team Meeting (30 min)

    a. Worship and prayer
    b. Personal message from Team Leader(s)
    c. Roll call
    d. Introduction of guests – non security team
    e. Introduction of new team members
    f. Announcements
    g. Any follow up from previous meeting
    h. Ask for mentor reports
    i. Ask: Anything new we should be thinking about
    j. Ask: Anything anyone wants to discuss since our last meeting
    k. Questions for clarification

Section 2: Worship and Security Team Classroom (30 min) – White Board & Markers

    1. SOGs for this training
        a. 1.1 - Membership
        b. 3.1 – Protocol
        c. 4.1 – Assignments/backup
        d. 5.1 – Chain of command
        e. 6.1 - Communications
        f. 7.1 - Actions
        g. 9.1 – Media communications

Section 3: Worship Security Team Practical (60 min)

    a. 4.1 - Reactions
    b. 6.1 - Communications
    c. 7.1 - Actions

Meeting/Training Agenda filed with Roll Call Attendance
Again, section one is more of a team communications segment. We always start with an opening prayer, followed by any message our team leaders wish to convey. Praising successful operations can boost morale and instill confidence. Maybe there is an event coming up that everyone needs to be made aware of. We also like to ask for prayer requests.

Roll call is important. Along with tightening up the security team with SOGs comes some paperwork that the church should insist on for liability reasons. If your church has no training in writing, there is no evidence of instruction or understanding by the people who comprise your security team.

Once a person attends training and is instructed with your churches written SOGs, there is evidence that you assessed your risks, strategically planned SOGs, trained your teams, and set expectations. Team members who break protocol can be asked to explain in more detail why they made a certain choice. They can be provided with focused instruction, disciplined or dismissed from the team and be provided with direct evidence of the breach or protocol, which will overcome claims of unfairness or discrimination, etc. which also protects the church from liabilities that can be associated with corrective actions.

Of course, introductions are important as are announcements. Asking for questions from previous training allows for clarification and better understanding. And, mentor reports are meant to let everyone know the progress a new team member is making. But the next two items are very important.

Asking the team if there is anything new we should be thinking about, allows team input and may identify opportunities missed in risk assessments, prior planning, training, etc.

Everyone likes to feel like they are part of the team and many like to have input on issues or discussions that they may not be listed on the agenda. Sometimes, it's feelings that are incomplete in regard to recent incidents that may have been handled in a different way.

Soon, we will be discussing energy flow of individuals and crowds. The best way I can explain this now is to imagine your favorite sports team playing a great game against a rival opponent. They are at home, their winning, it's not even close. The crowd is going wild, cheering, clapping, and screaming. The energy is high. You can sense that it's positive. You may even begin to feel sorry for the poor suckers playing on the opposing team. Then, midway through the game, the opposition comes alive through some miracle. They gain points. Your team starts making mistakes. The crowd quiets as the energy has just changed and you can feel it – even if you're not at the event.

We see this with response teams too. When confidence is shaken, when protocol is broken by accident, when a person who never should have gotten close to the pastor is standing in the front row during services and security has been breached – team energy can change quickly. You can see it on everyone's face. Disbelief turns to fear. Some team members will take this personally and assume responsibility. Anyone who has served in battle, in the military, as police, firefighting, and EMS knows exactly what I'm talking about. It's called Critical Incident Stress.

Emergency responders have a program called "Critical Incident Stress Debriefing." Just like soldiers who see humanity and destruction at its worst, responders experience things that can cause post-traumatic stress, also known as PTSD. Joseph A. Davis, Ph.D AUTHOR of "Crimes and Misdemeanors," wrote an article on CISD titled "Critical Incident Stress Debriefing From a Traumatic Event; Post Traumatic Stress following a Critical Incident" - Posted Feb 12, 2013.

"Caught off guard and numb from the impact of a critical incident, employers and employees are often ill-equipped to handle the chaos of such a catastrophic event like workplace violence. Consequently, survivors of such an event often struggle to regain control of their lives to regain a sense of normalcy. Additionally, many who have been traumatized by a critical life-changing event may eventually need professional attention and care for weeks, months and possibly years to come. The final extent of any traumatic event may never be known or realistically estimated in terms of loss, bereavement, mourning and grief. In the aftermath of any critical incident, psychological reactions are quite common and are quite predictable. Critical Incident Stress Debriefing or CISD and the management of traumatic reactions by survivors can be a valuable tool following a life-threatening event."

Keeping the energy of the team positive requires team leaders to constantly be measuring team dynamics. One tool used in CISD management is immediate feedback from team members involved, though we don't always have that opportunity. Typically, CISD meetings occur within 24 hours of a CISD incident. Hence, one of the last items on our agenda is to ask if anyone wants to discuss anything since our last meeting. Possibly, we're meeting a little late, but it's better than never addressing it.

Of course, team leaders should establish good communication with the team and allow team members to contact them at any time. Mistakes are made. We openly admit them when they happen, look for fixes so it doesn't happen again, and then we move past them. We highlight the mistakes in training and address them, because we learn from mistakes more than we learn from successes. Leaders instill and promote confidence and encourage high morale. We treat our teams the same Christlike way we treat our congregants.

Section two is all about classroom. Be aware of time elements and respect team member's free time. Our training sessions last for ninety minutes. We start and end on time. SOGs are very important, but we really only cover a few of the SOGs at every training. I usually hope to talk about more, but there's never enough time to cover everything I had planned for.

Reference was made in the agenda cited to "Draw up positions" as outlined in SOG 4.1. This was a reminder for me to make sure we had a dry erase board. Several handouts were also included. Team members received a copy of the SOGs and a copy of the training agenda. Additional copies of everything are available upon request and available in the security team office any time.

Practical training should be held in the sanctuary and in areas defined as a possible exposure in the risk assessment. This is a live training exercise based on the classroom portion. Classroom complements the practical and practical complements the classroom. Outside people may be invited to participate. I have included ushers, greeters, and even team members' children in our practical training. Include ushers, pastors, greeters, and other ministries in the training.

Eventually, we will discuss evacuation planning which, when called for in a real world situation, will include people from these other ministries as well.

Also, I've been approached by more people than I would have imagined, who have indicated they carry concealed weapons. They wanted me to know, they have my back. Well, they may find value in training with the team too. These people may also present a good recruiting opportunity as they are acting as sheepdogs anyway.

Notice that the classroom portion and the practical have the same SOGs. SOG 4.1 describes security post assignments and will detail backup positions (more on assignments later). I wrote, "Reactions," next to the practical part to remind me that one goal is to demonstrate how individual team members will respond to certain threats.

There are a variety of things to discuss when talking about a response. Obviously, the greater the depth of the response, the greater the variation of responses from team members will be. Preparing for a critical response where adrenalin is soaring, people may be running, screaming, crying, yelling, and sirens, alarms, and sprinklers may be going off. Power could be lost, radio headsets are filled with useless chatter, half garbled messages contain bad directions, and people who have nothing to with the incident are trying to get your attention. Outside responders come in and utter chaos ensues until someone with authority takes over and the incident stress level is relieved. Some things you can't train for, it's what comes with experience.

During my tenure training firefighters at my department, my cohort and good friend David made a suggestion that we adopted without seeking permission. We were the leaders for our department's technical rescue teams. I was also the extrication officer and he was the dive team leader. He suggested that we use a video camera on the heavy rescue truck that responded to car accidents and rescue calls that required any type of heavy mechanics, to record department responses to actual incidents. The goal was to video tape responses to identify areas of opportunity and gear training to correct problems.

During a call for a 10/50 PI, commonly known as a car accident with personal injuries, David decided to put his idea into practice. A vehicle, traveling on a county highway at 55 miles per hour or more missed a curve in the road and hit the side stone building. Slight extrication was performed and the two senior citizens were successfully removed from the crashed car.

As the video starts, we see the male driver of the car lying on a stretcher. He's properly attached to a long board with spider straps, all placed correctly. He's covered with a hospital blanket and the restraint belts are in place as they should be. The patient is wearing a neck collar and foam blocks were applied to stabilize his neck. It was a sunny warm afternoon and the patient was lying still, squinting to keep the sun out of his eyes.

Some firefighter found the patient's chest to be a good place to lay his helmet, which stayed there for a while, until the guy was loaded into the ambulance. However, the stretcher at some point was unattended…by anyone. The closest person was at least 15 feet away when the gurney began to slowly roll out of the parking lot area and into the street. As the camera panned to follow the moving cot, it caught the man's wife sitting on the tailboard of the back of the ambulance – also unattended, her hurt ankle not stabilized.

A few of us began yelling that the cot was moving, and it was picking up speed, but what I'll never forget is the look on the wife's face as she realized it was her husband that was rolling past her. It was a look of shock and disbelief.

The cot was stopped before it reached the street and the woman received treatment for her ankle. Everyone survived, the area was cleared, the car was towed, and the business repaired damages and reopened.

The video was used at the next extrication training and was meant to improve our response and on –scene actions.

Our department, like many others, is and continues to be a very well trained team. Certainly I'm not chronicling the thousands of incidents we responded to that went off without a hitch. The point is, things happen that we don't plan. Team members respond differently. Distractions are abundant. But, we learn best from our mistakes. We should not fear making mistakes, but we should try and limit making mistakes to making them while training.

I don't know if it was my critique of a different squad, or if people were really embarrassed by the video, but the Chief saw it differently. He saw potential liability claims if filming continued at different calls. David asked him, "So, if the video didn't exist and there was a liability claim, would you deny responsibility?"

I include this story here, because this incident happened sometime in the 1990's. Cell phones were not what they are today. Now, everyone has a camera and we should always imagine that whatever we're doing, we are being recorded somewhere.

People will record services in your church. They will use electronic devices to follow biblical passages in sermons. And they will be recording. The best way to avoid or reduce liability claims is to adopt SOGs, train, and enforce SOGs. Higher expectations must become part of the Esprit de corps of the group where excellence is the goal.

Since this book is also about the obstacles faced while trying to redevelop and grow a new team, this story has an amazing parallel.

After writing the first SOGs, I was told by church leadership that the church did not want SOGs. Like my chief, the reason given was that the church needed "plausible deniability." They felt SOGs were more of a liability and did not see the greater benefits.

"Plausible deniability," is the ability claim you should not be held liable or responsible, because the thing you are avoiding didn't have any written instruction, and thus you were unaware it was going on. This was a defense started by the CIA in the late 1980's, when Colonel Oliver North testified in the Iran-Contra scandal. It is not a good defense against liability claims and it is basically a lie. This also follows the opening story about churches that do not have a recognized security team, but are aware of individuals that perform this function. Be very aware that lack or SOGs or training does not eliminate or limit liability - quite the contrary.

If I can document that standards are employed with detailed operating guidelines or procedures, and that the person who violated those guidelines was trained on a regular basis in the application and expectations of the team and the church, I believe we eliminate dumb mistakes, individual assessment based on fear, and offer much better de-escalation potential.

When the team is trained according to our SOGs, which have been approved by our insurance company, I welcome anyone who wants to record our actions.

Time, after time, in today's violent divided society, we see people recording police actions. Yes, there are cases where a law enforcement officer is doing something wrong and that person deserves to be reprimanded or terminated, but we also see good officers exonerated and their names restored. Likewise, people with cameras I their cars can provide evidence that they are not at fault for accidents and even moving violations they may have been ticketed for.

Two important aspects to remember:

1) Training for larger incidents and reinforcing SOGs constantly will help your team when the real stuff hits the proverbial fan. Adrenalin, our body's "fight or flight," mechanism can set in quickly. Side effects may include: loss of hearing, loss of memory, PTSD, nausea, vomiting, spontaneous defecation, anxiety, slow motion time, tunnel vision and more.

Fear isn't really something you can practice. The kind of danger you may have to be in, to experience an adrenaline rush, can't be duplicated in a safe training environment. Reactions in a survival situation will be somewhat unpredictable and while accounts of traumatic incidents may have similarities, no two are the same.

Preparing and training, including practical training, for the confusion inherent in high stress responses will help guide team members to have some sort of minimal expectation hopefully making the incident more familiar and allowing them to better cope with the effects of adrenalin and offer a bit more clarity among all the confusion.

2) While live practical training is very important, it is never permissible to hold a surprise life and death training scenario with an un-expect-

ing live audience. Similarly, a drama team or skit in church should never make anyone believe they are in a life and death situation.

Many states allow individuals to conceal and carry firearms (CCW). Inciting an unsuspecting armed person could have fatal negative effects. Not to mention the potential detriment to any person with a heart condition or other medical problem that could be exacerbated by an adrenalin rush that causes their heart rate to escalate quickly.

Additionally, we don't want anyone in a real life and death situation to think they are seeing a training scenario or drama skit. There will never be a life and death training or skit in church during any service or function where people are gathered period!

This "guideline" is shared with all pastors, staff, volunteers, and congregants. When someone sees something that is not right, we want their first response to be alerting us and calling 911. For this reason we add:

NO TRAINING WILL EVER OCCUR PRIOR TO, DURING, OR IMMEDIATELY AFTER ANY CHURCH SERVICE OR AT ANY FUNCTION WHERE THE GENERAL PUBLIC IS INVITED TO THE CHURCH.

NO DRAMA MINISTRY SKIT WILL EVER INCLUDE A LIFE OR DEATH SCENERIO PRIOR TO, DURING OR IMMEDIATELY FOLLOWING ANY FUNCTION WHERE THE GENERAL PUBLIC IS INVITED TO CHURCH.

Chapter 5

PROTOCOL

Protocol is a general term that may define several operational aspects of a business, organization, team, etc. These are the rules, formalities, rituals, the thing to do, that encompasses everything from membership to training, behavior and dress to task execution. It will include basic protocols where the expectation is they will be followed every step of the way.

All employees in a company, or volunteers on a team should act in a uniform manner. For our volunteer security team, we have developed a specific church etiquette to achieve team objectives that are directly in line with the church's stated goals. Protocol helps to ensure that all employees/volunteers understand their role, the tasks and challenges they face, and how to execute them as quickly and accurately as possible.

Our team training provides protocol/etiquette exercises for our volunteers and includes other ministries that complement or rely upon our mission. These trainings may occur at another location or on-site. An increasingly diverse team requires such training to help people from all walks of life communicate with each other and work together.

Protocols help present a uniform, professional face to the public, church staff and volunteers. These protocols may unite team members under common goals and ensure that tasks are executed to the preferences of the church directors or according to church mission, goals, and vision. Confusion is eliminated and volunteers may be trusted to perform tasks quickly and independently. Team members who are presented with a ministry's protocols and etiquette up front will be able to make informed decisions about whether the position is right for them.

3.1 Church Worship Protocol

Protocol SOG:

1. VST members are expected to arrive at least thirty (30) minutes prior to the service they are volunteering for and stay at least 15 minutes after services have completed.

2. Notify team leader when late arrival or early leave is necessary.

3. Dress code: Unless otherwise indicated, VST members must wear the specified team attire/identification.
    a. No torn, stained, or unkempt clothing is allowed.

4. Sign in attendance book for each service.
    a. Team members will know their assignments.
    b. Assignments may be changed at any time by team leadership.

5. Assignments may be changed for special events.

6. Check out a radio and an ear piece.
    a. Radios need to be worn and "on" throughout VST member's time of service.
    b. Radios are to remain on campus, unless requested for an off campus event.

7. Team Leader will designate assignments.
    a. Report to assigned post.
    b. Leadership may reassign different areas before, during, and after services.

8. Five (5) minutes prior to service start team leaders will call for a position check.
    a. Position check order: see 4.1 Assignments.

9. Report any incidents and complete required documentation.

10. Turn in radio and ear piece at the end of shift. Report any broken or missing equipment.

11. Sign out.

3.2 VST EMS Protocol:

1. Arrive 30 minutes prior to event start.
2. Stay at least 15 minutes after event end.
3. Check equipment in first-aid bag.
4. Check AED battery.
5. Respond to any requests from anywhere on campus.
6. Assure all paperwork is completed for any incidents.
7. Restock first-aid bag.

While this may seem like real basic information, some might even suggest it's just common sense, but building the SOGs is much more than a few lines of "do's and don'ts." Together, these protocols make the next step in the security process easier to achieve. I.e.; our first goal is to "Deter." Once a threat has gone past deterrence, we can never totally go back. I'm not comfortable believing a hidden security force would help achieve this goal, even with the presence of identifiable team members. If undercover security worked better at deterrence, police would not wear uniforms.

Measuring the success of our deterrence protocols would include fewer worship disruptions; fewer security reports, fewer incidents, but we'll never know how effective we really are. Only in the mind of the person posing a potential threat can deterrence effectiveness be measured. Our success is obvious when nothing happens.

Without an initial deterrence baseline created by our presence, more individual threats and disruptions will get through what should be a first line of defense. Once that threat comes through the door and finds a seat, the deterrence opportunity is gone and we start from a weaker position.

Without SOGs, protocols, and training each team member is basically left to make up their own decisions – which should scare anyone without any further detail. Team cohesiveness may be missing, resulting in missed reactions. No organized response requires each team member to make quick assumptions that may not be in line with desired results. No drills to reinforce liability awareness may leave the church and individuals on the VST open to law suits. No plan for larger incidents that require outside agencies to respond could put more people in harm's way, jeopardize outside agencies reaction time, foul crime scene evidence, and fail to address immediate issues, like saving lives.

Yes, I do trust myself. I trust that every one of our team members has their heart in the right place. I believe that any actions we would take, in our mind, would be the best decision we would imagine for the church. But your decision and my decision in the same circumstances may not even be close to similar.

Incidents don't usually take a lot of time to unravel; in fact they tend to explode in the moment. If you're lucky, you might have a few seconds to make a response after your mind comprehends what it is witnessing. Establishing written protocols before an incident offers guidelines.

Think of instance where your volunteer team leader is not available, the new guy on the team that has never experienced any type of interruption, or when the person you brought onto the team is the person causing the problem. What happens next?

What happens when the person stealing tithes is on the security team? What do your protocols say about someone you've known for years who is found by your team sexually abusing a child?

What about that wannabe police officer? You know...the person who had just a few too many psychological concerns for the police academy to hire him. What happens when they begin to escalate a bad situation just to prove their selves? What will your protocol be and who will enforce it?

These issues can also place additional burdens on the church in the form of liability claims. Congregants can react similarly and open the church to same potential law suits. As I said earlier in the book, your church may not have an established security team…but there is probably someone or some people playing the part, ready to make a decision on their own to handle a situation that no one was expecting.

Once an incident is occurring, our role is to "De-escalate" the interruption and keep people safe. If we haven't established SOGs, communications, chain of command, and protocols before the incident occurs, achieving de-escalation could be a lot tougher.

Finally, after an incident we may hold critical stress debriefing sessions to determine what happened, where we failed, and where we succeeded. We may identify areas of opportunity for growth and other enhancements like back up, positions we need covered, response protocols, etc.

Standardizing SOGs will also help with recruiting. People like to volunteer and they like direction and structure. It is far more difficult getting people to volunteer when they don't know what the expectations are.

Happy people will also stick around longer and team retention will be higher. But equally important is the leadership succession pool that is created. When a leader steps down, the church and the team must be able to fill the void quickly. With this system in place, SOGs do not need to be recreated every time a new person takes over. It provides a uniform training for all new members and then allows pastors to identify leaders.

We started this SOG with a dress code. There are many opinions out there regarding team members being uniformed or plain clothes. My personal feeling was that uniformed security was not really needed in the sanctuary during services; however it was apparent that there was a need for some type of team identification. Due to the number of team members and future goals, uniform shirts were a bit expensive.

Researching "Church Security (lapel) Pins," we found a white shield with a red Knights of St. John or Crusaders cross lapel pin. The Maltese cross has always been special to me because of the Templar Knights and their Maltese cross that also represents firefighters. Each church is unique in its needs and will have to examine how they feel is the best way for their security team to dress or be identified.

Know that pins are easy to lose, and so the team director should have extras available for team members who show up without a pin.

As we started to see our team expand, we decided to search for a different pin. We now wear a gold and red pin with a crusader, sword and shield that says, "Put on the full armor of God." It has had a better reception by the team. It also added a new dimension to our team as people are commenting on the pins and asking how they can get one. The answer is easy, "Join the team."

Pin identification has been very successful. Greeters, ushers, pastors, and even congregants know who we are and what we are doing. They feel safer knowing they can approach us with questions, concerns, or to help. Because of our success, church leadership has embraced this identifier and team morale has increased.

My church security experience started at a different church a few years ago. Team members could wear whatever they wanted. But, it was a very tight team, very well organized. Their identifier was a plastic picture card attached to a lanyard. It had the team member's name on it and clearly said security. There was one other difference – the lanyard is red, compared to the lanyards of all other ministries, which are black. So, usually, pastors, ministries, and congregants could easily identify who was security.

Identification of security team members is also important during incidents where local police/fire, FBI, Homeland Security and other outside agencies may be called in. We have initiated one new protocol and are working on the second.

Recently we added an incident command IC) board. This is a magnetic, white dry erase board. Every Team Member has their own magnetic name tag that is attached to the board when they arrive. The IC system identifies Team Leaders by color, and contains the names of everyone on the team that is present. This system complies with FEMA 100 and 700 Incident command system guidelines. In a situation where outside agencies respond, we can plug our team into any responding agencies IC system, as they all follow FEMA 100 – 800 IC protocols.

We would plug in under the Resources manager and could be used for activities such as guiding satellite news trucks or managing people flocking to the church to pray.

Currently, we are working on adding a step in the protocol SOG that would require every team member to wear a pouch containing a sash when they are actively performing their duties. The sash has big letters in reflective orange that say, "SECURITY." No one would see this in any situation except in a larger scenario where outside agencies are called in. The sash is folded into a pouch and easily deployed. Team members put it on very simply and would leave it on until instructed by the team leader to remove them.

Again, SOGs are always changing. The sash costs about $40 each and we'll have to have discussions about the costs and benefits. As I'm writing this, I have a meeting tonight with a group of security leaders from the east valley of Phoenix. I will also share this with tem to see if anyone has experience with this and get feedback that I can take back to my teams and church decision makers.

In a two week period our team picked up three new team members. They could be assigned to posts where regulars (congregants who sit in the same seats every service) don't recognize them. Remember, the first goal is to deter. Having a security presence that is not identified does not provide the level of deterrence desired. It's kind of like telling the threat, we're here and our plan is to trick you into doing something you might choose not to do if you could see that we really do have a response to your devious plans. That's great, but it's predicated upon responding. Excellence requires that our plans always be proactive – every step of the way.

Security team members stand at their post and observe the crowd. Whoever we see can usually see us too. Admittedly, I already look suspicious, because I'm acting like the type of person we want to try to detect – always moving our heads, being on the lookout for someone who isn't fitting in the crowd as opposed to the person who is a potential threat, often moving their head, looking around to see who is watching.

Our attention is usually away from the object that everyone else is looking at. When everyone is looking forward at the pastor, we are looking back, across, and from side to side in our goal to detect a person of interest, someone who could be a potential threat.

It can't be repeated often enough, because typically untrained volunteers are looking for the scary person, which is a judgement. A "bad" person, or a person with "bad" intentions, gets into our "good" space by acting how they believe a "good" person would act. Their biggest enemy in being detected early is themselves. They worry that they will make a mistake in their walk, actions, speech, etc, and will be detected early, which would foil their plot, whatever it is. And so, they look around to see who is watching, count how many watchers there are and where they are positioned. And most important, if they have been detected, who is coming for them and where are they coming from. There is no judgement here, just the observation that this person does not fit a baseline behavior. Nothing about their race, age, heritage, economic status, etc., is applied. This is purely based on actions they take as they climb the proverbial ladder to achieving their goal.

Security team members who "roam," move around quite a bit, which is a normal church activity. Assessing the crowd to detect who the threat may be, we first have to establish a baseline of activity for the entire group, which in this case is basically looking forward at what is on the stage. We'll get into more detail when we talk about team actions, but basically anyone who doesn't fit the baseline activity of the group would raise suspicions, just as our security team will also raise suspicions of individuals who subconsciously notice we are going against the baseline.

Sometimes, especially if I'm a "roamer," my stride may be too fast for the baseline environment I'm in. When I'm standing at an entrance I'm looking at details that a predator or threat might also look at before picking a victim, which again stands out against the baseline of people smiling, saying good morning, and looking ahead as they walk in to church.

Point is, security will stand out. And, when people feel that vibe that something isn't fitting in this picture they look at us just as they would look at anything that struck them as out of place or odd. Their faces appear riddled. If they had time, they'd probably want to know who we are and what we're doing. This is another reason identification is so important.

Problem is, most people are not in touch with their senses. They drop their defenses and allow bad people into their safety zone. After all, this is church and we are Christians, what could possibly happen at church? But it's bad guys who act like good guys that make their way into our safety zone. And, because they know they are bad guys disguised as good guys, they are not 100% confident in their ability to fool everyone. There are giveaways in their actions that are obvious when measured against the baseline of our congregation.

While our church does have uniformed security on our campus, they do not provide protection for worship services. In fact, they pretty much avoid the main church building during services. Some feel that uniformed security has the appearance that things have gotten to the point where uniformed security is needed, and that that's not the message most churches want to send.

A few decades ago, before cell phones, I was an armed security guard as a side job. The firm I worked for was hired by a large toy retailer to guard the cash registers around Christmas time. Hundreds of thousands of dollars flowed through the registers daily. Certainly, it could be a prime target for thieves. So, I was hired as a deterrent.

One day, a store manager asked me if I would shoot anyone who tried to rob the place. My response was simple. I pointed to the exit and asked if he could see those doors. He nodded yes and I told him that's where I'd be if something happened, which I would imagine most security guards would do.

Typically, they are not paid enough to put their lives on the line and most likely, they're not members of the company or church they work for. Today we see advertisements for LifeLock Inc., (an American identity theft protection company), portray scenes where people we believe are there to react to our immediate needs claim to be nothing more than deterrents or warning systems. The same is true of most uniformed security.

Some churches mix their security and have both uniformed and plain clothes members in the sanctuary during services. Again, you will want to look at your risk factors, membership composition, and address assessment goals. For most churches, uniformed security is cost prohibitive.

Though our team is discernable by the ear bud we wear, not everyone is familiar with that. So, we designed lapel pins that stick out. We just purchased fifty pins for one hundred and fifty dollars. We've talked about team shirts, identification badges with our pictures on them, and other recognition garb, but this pin seems to work very well. It gives us presence, without being overbearing.

What really helps us is the church "grapevine." You know how fast rumors and information flow faster than the Internet? Well, the same is true of our team. It's not us telling people we're security, its members telling members and that's a great way to build the feeling of security. We are a very large mega church and I lost count of how many people I didn't know have approached us and asked if we were security. Quite a few times this question was followed by a need that we could help with including: lost children, lost personal items, directions, EMS, and advice for those seeking more personal help.

This is also a great opportunity to introduce ourselves, share more of the church's missions, and outreach services.

Recently, it was decided that the Security team be issued black Tommy Bahama style shirts with an embroidered church logo and the word "Shepherd," stitched in Red on a black shirt. We thought it would make us look sharp. We never adopted it, but if uniformity is important to your church, you may decide to try it.

It is important that people know who is in charge of certain emergencies or who it is that's asking people to leave their seats. Kids, teens, other congregants and their guests must feel free to approach us with concerns, for information, etc. We also find, there are a number of attendees who would love to lend a hand when the need arises – but someone has to be in charge that can instruct helpers as to our process for the incident at hand.

We are identifiable by some means and most people know we are providing security. Through this protocol, we establish command and the flock follows us.

John 10:27 My sheep listen to my voice; I know them, and they follow me. Another change in our new SOGs was that we initially had the idea of an assignment board that would be a lined board starting with #1 on top, followed on the next line with #2, then #3 and so on. When a team member arrived, they fill in the next available number and that is the position they are assigned. Well…this has now changed too.

Again, I'm keeping some of our changes over the first few months in the book so you can see the process we went through, what our thinking was, and how we explored opportunity, sought input from many resources, and dealt with change issues among team members.

Earlier, I wrote about our sign in book, a binder that is separated by month. Each month contains enough sign in sheets for the number of services held. Each team member signs in next to the first open position as we have determined these positions to be the most critical in order of importance. Feel free to change these around to meet your specific needs.

Back in the 1990s, the fire services had devised a team duty and hierarchy structure referred to as an "Accountability System." Volunteers were not assigned to specific trucks as they weren't stationed at the fire house and couldn't be counted upon to arrive in the strategic order we needed trucks to leave in.

The idea was that as volunteers arrived at the fire house, a firefighter would just fill the next open position on a truck. Trucks were dispatched in an exact order and specific assignments for firefighters and EMS were assigned to each truck. This, the first truck to arrive on-scene would be the initial attack truck with firefighters pulling hose lines and entering the structure, while the second truck was responsible for providing a water source from a hydrant or other source and would also bring a backup team to support the on the first truck.

Additional trucks would fill other roles in a descending order of importance.

If we waited for assigned crews to arrive before leaving the firehouse it would mess up the response order or cause great delays. We needed the attack truck to leave first; followed by a pumper, followed by more crew - usually our heavy rescue truck that held up to seventeen people, followed by the aerial ladder truck...you get the point. Each truck is built with specifications precisely for that truck's purpose. The first truck out of the firehouse was an attack truck, while the second truck out was a pumper. Importance was placed on strategic planning and positioning, based on best practices.

This is very similar to our approach of using a volunteer security team to sign in and cover the highest risk area first.

Since each truck had different firefighters on it, officers and engineers (drivers) didn't always know who showed up, what truck they were on, or if their crews were all present when leaving the scene to go back to the firehouse. I do remember more than a few occasions where a firefighter's truck had left them stranded on the scene and they had to find a ride back to the firehouse with a different rig and sometimes those vehicles were with an entirely different community's truck that was providing mutual aid to our department.

Here is where the idea of using security/EMS team members from different campuses, to fill security/EMS team assistance requests fits in. Campuses that may request this form of "mutual aid" need to be able organize the participating responders from different campuses.

Eventually, accountability systems meant each firefighter had two or three Velcro nametags attached to the inside of their helmet. When we boarded a truck, one tag went on a small "crew board," the second was handed to an officer prior to entering a building, fire or rescue scene and attached to a larger board that would indicate who was assigned to specific tasks and even who was resting. Most important, it let officers know who was in the burning building or danger zone. Some of you may be familiar with confined space lock-out tag-out processes and this is very similar.

At the end of the incident, as volunteers left the scene, their name tags were handed back to them. This was a great system for accountability. Likewise, regardless of your team size, officers needed to know who from the team was on site.

At the end of services, we need to know that the person/people providing security were accounted for. This also provides an attendance reference, possibly years down the road, for the churches attorney or insurance company, regarding volunteers who could be called upon to testify or bear witness about an event that occurred.

Benefits of using an accountability system include retaining a list of people who attended the response. Color coded name tags that are colored to indicate team directors, team leaders, EMS, and security team members. Everyone knows who is in charge and who could be next to run lead an incident response should team directors and team leaders become inaccessible.

As fighter fighters, All of this translated into better report writing and chain of command. But even more important, we knew who was supposed to be on which truck and we knew very quickly if someone didn't report back.

Accountability is now the process we use for our teams. Signing in means we know who is/was there. It helps in report writing. It's another piece of documentation an insurance company may request in an annual audit. But more important, if we should ever have a critical situation occur, we can account for each person who signed in. This information is available and can be shared with outside responders quickly. Of course you can alter this any way you want to fit your specific risk assessment plan, this is the original Worship Security Team Accountability sign in sheet:

Volunteer Security Team

Accountability Sheet

Date: _____

Service Time: _____

Security Positions Before/During Services

25 Minutes before services:

Position	Name
Door 1	
Door 1	
Door 2	
Door 3	
Door 4	
Sanctuary	
Sanctuary	

Positions during service:

Positions	Name	Radio Number
1 - Stage Left		
2 - Center Stage Area		
3 - Stage Right		
4 - Aisle 3 Back		
5 - Aisle 2 Back		
6 - Roam		
7 - Roam		
8 - Back Stage		
9 - EMS		
10 -		

We found it was easier to eliminate the "Positions" section, because every service provided a different need. Our upper balconies were closed on Wednesday and Saturday. Sunday's first service attendance was less than the second service. So we now use this simplified version:

Worship Security Team

Accountability Sheet

Campus: _____

Volunteer Security Team – Accountability Sheet

Date_____   Service Time_____

Name	Radio Number

Eventually, we switched back to our original Accountability sheet. Play around with different ideas and develop something that works best for your team.

Some team members had become set in their ways from years of doing security and developing their favorite position. They may come into church first and yet sign their name under position #4, leaving the top positions open.

We did work to accommodate in the past, but having all positions filled from #1 on down is most important, as the position numbering system addresses the most critical areas first.

If only one team member showed up, they would automatically be #1. We'll go through assignments in the next chapter in greater detail. But you can see that if the only person who showed up signed up for position #4, it would not address what we assessed as our most crucial position.

Our SOGs do provide that the team leader can readjust the assignment importance and switch out team members who may be able to better perform an assignment function. Assignments #1, #2, #3, and #4 directly relate to protecting the pastor.

Some churches allow firearms to be carried by team members, though your state and local gun laws will prevail. In more than a few churches I have attended, security team leaders prefer armed security positioned in front of the stage area near the pastor. If an unarmed team member were to sign their name to position near the pastor, a team leader could switch an armed team member who is not near the stage and reassign the unarmed team member to a different position. We will cover more on firearms in Chapter 10 – "Firearms," which should be called, "The Greatest Challenge."

I like things that flow smoothly. Part of this is having assignments filled and team members at their position at least 10 minutes prior to services. We complete an audible position confirmation over our radios starting with position #1, about 5 minutes before services start.

"This is Joe at position #1," followed by the next person & position on the list. This tells team leaders everyone is in place and ready. It also lets other security members know who is there and what positions they are in. Since positions dictate response, team members will know who to expect, should backup be required.

Leadership may assign different areas before, during, and after services. These would most likely be door positions or the event we want to focus on someone we detected as a person of interest. There could also be an after services activity we have been asked to watch over, like a baptism, meet and greet, or Easter egg hunt type event.

I'd like to write that, "almost certainly," we will not have a team member repeat the same assignment twice. And we understand that everyone needs to have the opportunity to be trained on all positions, but reality is, some people will always figure out a way to slip into the same position, time and time again.

You will find a copy of our Security and EMS reports in the appendix. Team members must fill out reports legibly, as full as possible, and on the day of the occurrence. Completed paperwork should be turned into the team leader and filed.

Team Director will decide on Critical Stress Incident Debriefing (CSID) sessions, based upon the nature of the disturbance or EMS call. Affected members of the team, team leaders, pastors, and others involved (ie: ushers) will be invited for a get together at the campus where the disturbance occurred. People directly affected by the disturbance will have time to recant their story and to talk about their feelings of the resulting actions. Additional steps may be taken by church authorities to assure affected people are treated in a timely manner.

3.2 Media Policy

Security team members may see and hear things that could make for some juicy gossip. A husband and wife arguing with no filters and things are said that could later be regretted, or you could find that the couple everyone admires is talking about divorce. A child comes up to you and says something about their home that any adult understands is not for public broadcast and has nothing to do with the welfare of the child. People come to church to find salvation and you just happen to be the person they decide to confess something to.

Sometimes things are caught on security cameras that are personal. Once in a while these private things may come up in training or as comments one morning when the team is getting their radios and putting on ear pieces, in talking with another team member, or on a report left in public view. As volunteers, we are also trustees of the church and must keep events, incidents, and gossip we are exposed to confidential.

Additionally, The Health Insurance Portability and Accountability Act of 1996 (HIPAA), was enacted on August 21, 1996. The HIPPA law establishes, for the first time, a set of national standards for the protection of certain health information. These standards address the use and disclosure of individuals' health information—called "protected health information."

Any group or organization that provides health care, including immediate EMS basic response, comes under the classification of "Business Associate." According to the U.S. Department of Health and Human Services, "In general, a business associate is a person or organization, other than a member of a covered entity's workforce, that performs certain functions or activities on behalf of, or provides certain services to, a covered entity that involve the use or disclosure of individually identifiable health information."

Civil penalties for not protecting a patient's right to privacy could range from $100 to $50,000 or more – per incident, up to $1,500,000 per year. "A person who knowingly obtains or discloses individually identifiable health information in violation of the Privacy Rule may face a criminal penalty of up to $50,000 and up to one-year imprisonment. The criminal penalties increase to $100,000 and up to five years imprisonment if the wrongful conduct involves false pretenses, and to $250,000 and up to 10 years imprisonment if the wrongful conduct involves the intent to sell, transfer, or use identifiable health information for commercial advantage, personal gain or malicious harm. The Department of Justice is responsible for criminal prosecutions under the Privacy Law." And none of this includes potential civil liability claims from the individual(s) whose information was shared.

Once in a while, our security team will respond to an EMS call on campus. We have EMS reports that contain a lot of personal information. These should be filed in a locked file cabinet where only team leaders have access. These records may be shared with EMS responders at the time of the incident.

Find your state's requirements for how long these files need to be kept. Double check with your church attorney as records are kept as evidence for potential liability suits which may be brought against the church years down the road.

After the requisite time for holding the files is past, they should be shredded and disposed.

Some time ago, a woman had a seizure in one of our bathrooms. I was the first person to respond from our church. Upon arrival, she was unresponsive. The bathroom was cleared. A nurse from our congregation joined me. Fire department EMS was called.

I got her name from a prescription bottle in her purse. We assessed the medication to determine she most likely had epilepsy and suffered a seizure. We monitored vital signs and interviewed a witness. A doctor from the congregation joined us and took over immediate care. As I was moving away from the scene, EMS arrived. The woman did not suffer any additional injuries and was in church again the next week.

As I walked back into the hallway, which is about thirty feet wide, pastors, staff, volunteers, and congregants began asking questions. "Who is it?" "What happened?" "Will she be alright?" All I could relay was that, "She was in good hands and they are taking good care of her. Now is a good time to pray."

In other incidents, it may be natural for people in your church to congregate around the patient and pray. Be careful, because EMS responders, including outside agencies, will begin asking personal health history questions immediately.

Imagine, the second question asked is, "What happened to you?" What if the response is very embarrassing and overheard by a well-meaning parishioner? Again, this could become a liability. Be sure and clear people out of the working area, away from the patient.

Sharing personal health information with anyone outside of the "need–to-know" loop could open the church to a liability suit.

Because we strive to operate in a Christ-like fashion, these things that we witness must be kept confidential. Throughout this book and in my personal life I try to always remember to respect the privacy of others. This book is filled with stories from my church and firefighting days. Except where I purposefully used names, you would never know who was involved in these stories. These things we see and hear should never be repeated outside of our team and our church pastors. Teams should strictly forbid retelling these things on social media as well. Anything repeated could result in a liability to the church on a community and/or financial level.

Someday your church may experience an issue that requires outside assistance, which could attract the attention of media. Additionally, the smaller the community you live in, the greater potential your incident will be reported and the greater possibility you will actually know who the reporter is. I've lived in a small community where students were cited for underage smoking off the high school grounds. It was a big story, and it doesn't take much to understand how big of a story a church incident would be.

It's important to remember that a reporter, even if they are a close friend, thrives on sensationalism and will be looking for some inside information. Remember that there is really nothing that is "Off the Record." Anything you say can be used, including your name, even when a promise of confidentiality is made.

Government entities, municipalities, police, fire departments, and many corporations employ highly trained media relations professionals who understand the media and know what to say to satisfy them, while at the same time working to maintain the integrity and mission of the entity they represent. Media relations specialists are responsible for moderating communications between the organization and various media outlets such as newspapers, radio broadcasts, television stations, and includes social media. Larger churches may employ a media relations specialist. Any statement you make could make you a material witness, even if what you are repeating is just hearsay. A material witness is a witness whose testimony or evidence is likely to be sufficiently important to influence the outcome of a trial – which can be used by either the prosecutor or the defense.

Regardless of your political views, anyone who watches television, listens to the radio, or reads print material has experienced the sensationalism of the media. Just reporting the news (if there is any) won't generate ratings as effectively as reporting news items with an emotional twist. Reporters often use meaningless one-dimensional statistics or make dramatic statements to get reaction.

Bias is another aspect of the news that has become more and more apparent over the years. Have you ever listened to a news story and thought it sounded one-sided? Or have you thought the news didn't seem to report the whole story or the most important aspect of a story? That could be a sign of media bias.

Over the past several years, we have seen mass shootings by one religious sect where the media has decided not to report on the terrorist's religious affiliations. Meanwhile, Christians are painted as "haters" of anyone whose life decisions are different than those followed in the Bible. Churches do not get the same considerations as the real villains. Every church should have a trained media professional who is capable of answering questions and handling reporters. This is the only person who should have authority to speak with the media.

Not included in the SOGs, but something we do cover in training because of its importance, is crime scene preservation.

Dena Weiss, professor of criminal justice at American Military University wrote: "The Crime Scene: Tips for How First Responders Can Help Preserve Key Evidence" which appeared in http://inpublicsafety.com/2014/08/the-crime-scene-tips-for-how-first-responders-can-help-preserve-key-evidence/ August 22, 2014.

She writes, "First responders to crime scenes are a crucial part of any criminal investigation. The first officer at the scene has many responsibilities including:

- Establishing the perimeter of the crime scene
- Determining where the suspect(s) entered and exited
- Keeping unauthorized people out of the crime scene"

In most cases, evidence should not be tampered with. First responders may take pictures to preserve evidence that may be disturbed by weather or other conditions.

"Crime Scenes are Fragile, be Conscious of Contamination.
In the past, contamination issues that CSI's were most concerned with included:

- Absence of personal protective equipment (PPE) such as gloves
- Officers leaving shoeprints in crucial areas of the scene
- Officers spitting or tossing cigarette butts within the scene
- Officers handling doors and windows that were a point of entry/exit by suspect(s)
- Officers handling electronic devices"

Remember, "Key evidence can be anywhere." Attend to those requiring medical aid, but try and keep people from entering the scene and disturbing evidence.

From our SOGs:

3.2 Talking to Media/Cameras/Posting to Social Media

1. Team members are also restricted from communicating or commenting on incidents on social media and are forbidden from posting, sharing, or replying to any posted verbiage, photographs or videos, including "like" or similar buttons.

Chapter 6

POSITION ASSIGNMENTS

4.1. Position Assignments

Assigned positions for all services and performances are as follows:
Someone will always be designated to shadow the Senior Pastor – this is a priority position. This is a "Personal Protection" position. The VST member performing this task may also accept a position assignment.

All other VST members will be assigned as follows:
1. 1st position: Aisle 1, front row.

2. 2nd position: Aisle 2, front row or close.

3. 3rd position: Aisle 3, front row or close.

4. 4th position: Aisle 4, front.
    a. Positions 1-4 are stationary, and do not provide backup.
5. 5th position: Aisle 3 rear.

6. 6th position: Aisle 2 rear.

7. 7th position: Roamer – Covers all areas of church sanctuary.

8. 8th position: Roamer – Covers all areas of church sanctuary.
   a. a. Positions 5-8 provide backup to any area.

9. 9th position: EMS – Locate anywhere, responds to medical calls only.

4.2 Pre & Post service door assignments
1. Door 1 – Main door west entrance.

2. Door 2 – Main door lower north entrance.

3. Door 3 – Upper mezzanine.

4. Door 4 - Upper mezzanine.

5. Roamer: Covers doors 1, 2, 3, and 4 of main church, mezzanine 1 and 2, all stairways, public and nonpublic areas, parking lots, child check in, administration building, other classes and buildings.

Assigned positions for all services and performances are as follows:
1. 1st position: Left side of stage – stationary.

2. 2nd position: Center stage - stationary.

3. 3rd position: Right Side of stage - stationary.

4. 4th position: Main floor, aisle 3, rear: provides backup to any position requesting it.

5. 5th position: Main floor, aisle 2, rear: provides backup to any position requesting it.

6. 6th position: 1st Mezzanine: full floor coverage including Door

3 and Door 4: provides backup for any position requesting it, including offerings escort.

7. 7th & 8th position: Roamer: Covers all areas of church sanctuary - provides backup for all positions, escorts offerings, includes "immediate" outside security.

8. 9th position: Backstage: provides backup to position 1, 2, and 3.

9. EMS: Responds to radio calls and may station anywhere in the church.

Security team members assigned to executive protection (EP) of church pastors will be assigned a specific objective and will follow protocols specific to the EP Team. EP team members will have the authority to direct team leaders and team members at any time.

These "Assignments" have been determined to be critical points of importance as the result of a security risk assessment, performed at least once annually. Due to their observational, reactional, and risk assessed advantage, it is imperative that team members hold their position until reassigned. They should not be allowed to decide their own changes.

Criminals, threats, predators, terrorists, whatever term we agree to use, barring intoxication, drug use, and psychological issues, may challenge security looking for weaknesses. Any hole in protection may be noticed and breached, making predesigned plans difficult to complete and put team, church, and service attendees at risk. Your team positions will vary according to your risk assessment; this is an example of how positions flow with prioritization.

Early in the SOG implementation phase, position #1 was assigned to shadow the pastor. We ran into a few difficulties with the team being able to follow an assignment numbering system that was not logical or easy to understand, because #1 was a moving position. One of our team leaders suggested a simpler system that we adopted, that labeled positions from the left side of the stage and progressed in a clockwise manner around the sanctuary covering the most vital points according to our risk assessment.

Removing the "shadow" security position number provided an opportunity to create a detailed unit who are assigned to protect pastors directly, providing personal security services. Some of our personal security team also travels with their pastor when they are on other campuses appearing in person.

Since shadow assignment positions or personal protection for pastors are fairly permanent, as opposed to regular team assignments, there is no longer an assignment number for this team. These team members also have their own chain of command and SOGs, not included in this book. They do not wear team identification, and cannot be reassigned to a different task, unless the pastor they are shadowing is not in attendance.

Creating assignment positions demands recognition and triage style grading of assessed risks. At a mass casualty incident, a system of triage must be utilized to determine who will receive treatment in order of potential for survival versus those who may have perished or have a low potential for survival, and of those receiving treatment, who can wait and who goes first.

Triage Levels use "Color Coding," a color-coded tagging method to categorize disaster victims in the field has been almost universally adopted and incorporated into existing triage systems.

Numeric values are color coded and each patient (risk) is assessed.

- Red Triage Tag ("Immediate" - Priority 1): Patients lives are in immediate danger and require immediate treatment;
- Yellow Triage Tag ("Delayed" - Priority 2): Patients lives are not in immediate danger and will require urgent, not immediate, medical attention;
- Green Triage Tag ("Minimal" - Priority 3): Patients with minor injuries who may eventually require treatment;
- Black Triage Tag ("Expectant" - No Priority): Patients are either dead or have such extensive injuries that they cannot be saved.

Data from federal, state, and local response agencies like the Federal Bureau of Investigation (FBI), Department of Homeland Security (DHS), sheriff's department, local police, etc. may help in the risk analysis and assignment decision making process. A majority of security responses will most likely be for medical emergencies and small disruptions, which will come from the audience.

Greater emphasis is placed on watching the crowd and open entrances, rather than remote, typically unused entrances. It doesn't mean there is no risk with an unlocked stage door or basement entrance; just that the people attending worship tend to be the more immediate place a disruption would occur.

If volunteers were numerous, funds overflowing, and resources abundant, we could cover everything. Do I really need to finish this seemingly impossible thought?

Positions closer to the top of our "Accountability Sheet" are ranked higher in importance. Since volunteer teams are not always fully staffed, it is expected that prioritized positions will be covered first, based upon the goals of the ministry. Again, our first goal is to protect the pastor. Then, we work our way out and expand our perimeter of coverage.

A few months ago, during a Wednesday night service, a tall middle aged man walked from the back of the sanctuary all the way to where the pastor was sitting in the front row. Our main floor holds about three thousand five hundred seats…it's not a short walk. He was carrying flowers, which was odd to begin with, but no one even saw him until he was right next to our lead pastor.

The team jumped when they realized this guy was talking to the pastor and interrupting the service. A chase ensued. The threat exited through doors that only usually had lighter traffic as most people used a different main door. Radio communications instructed the team to respond to the wrong door. Every single security team member was off their posts and the church, pastor, and congregation were no longer being watched. The threat jumped into his pickup truck and left. He has never returned.

Immediately after the incident, team members began to realize that a potential threat was able to make his way down the long aisle, past ushers, past security, and past a taped off area before being seen. Realizing the potential threat, team members wondered aloud, what if the threat had a knife or a gun. And the critical incident stress began to set in. That's what happens when team members begin to imagine what could have been and the reality that no one was trained to respond.

Suddenly the team started to realize there was zero security in the sanctuary and there was a hustle to get back to make sure there was no secondary attacker.

This one small incident was the main catalyst for these SOGs. It was a great learning experience. Here's another great lesson – make your mistakes in training sessions – not during services. Train assigned positions. Any team member should be able to take on any assignment and be able to follow SOGs. When a team member takes a position that is to be stationary, and they move from that position, it must be clear that they now allow a threat the opportunity of a vulnerable position.

After 9/11, FEMA came out with a training guide for fire departments responding to terrorist threats. It talked about the acronym "BNICE," which stands for, Biological, Nuclear/Radiological, Incendiary, Chemical, and Explosive Agents. The training class for this program discusses in great detail the potential for secondary attacks and to always be on the alert. This concept must be applied to church security as well. When a primary incident occurs the team must be vigilant and be on the watch for a secondary disrupter.

One last note regarding assignments: Remember - teams should always conduct themselves as if they're always on camera, because they most likely will be. In addition to church cameras recording services and surveillance cameras, almost everyone in the crowd has a phone or tablet capable of recording and sharing on social media with the click of a button.

Chapter 7

CHAIN OF COMMAND

5.1 Chain of Command

1. Lead Executive Director oversees all campuses and the VST.

2. VST Director (TD) oversees all activities of the VST and will serve as Incident Commander until turned over to an outside agency.

3. EMS Director oversees all activities of the VST/EMS, including record maintenance for certifications and/or licenses of EMS members, assigns EMS members to regular events and as requested, communicates supply needs, and maintains equipment. EMS Director is Incident for all EMS calls, until relinquished to an outside agency.

4. VST and EMS Team Leader (TL) is assigned to lead the VST/EMS at a specific service or event and is responsible for prioritizing team member assignments and assures all team goals are met. VST TL assumes command when Directors are not present.

5. VST Assistant Team Leader (ATL) will help TL and will assume command when TD and TL are not present. ATL will fill function as TL when designated TL is not present.

6. VST/EMS Member: is a member of the church congregation in good standing, Greets worshippers warmly, always on the alert for people of interest, disrupters, intruders, vandals, etc. Follows the SOGs of deter, delay, detect, deny, respond to and recover from loss events, and assist calling emergency medical services when needed. Communicates all facts to team members. Follows orders of Team Leader and may be designated as Team Leader when requested.

7. EMS members: Will respond to medical incidents, assess and provide proper treatment commensurate with their level of certification/licensing. Document incident on the proper form, and assist the security team where capable.

8. Should TD, TL, and ATL not be available, the following position order will determine TL and if necessary, incident command: P11, P10, P9, P6, P5, P8, P7, P4, P3, P2, and P1.

9. EMS – EMS is leader at all EMS responses.

10. Organizational structure will dictate your chain of command. This was a big headache as we were establishing the team. I have purposefully removed my church's name from this book, because of the pushback our team has received from the command chain.

It is with good intention that old SOGs have been included in some instances in this book to demonstrate changes we have made as better processes are found. By making he effort to continually seek best practices and being open to new methods, our goal should always be to protect every aspect of our mission as best we can. We take on the responsibility of protecting our church, its pastors, staff, volunteers, congregation, and visitors, but we also have a responsibility to protect our team.

That being said, our old chain of command SOGs were based upon my understanding of the church hierarchy. Including these church staff members seemed politically expedient in achieving my personal goal getting the SOGs passed. It was felt that by including "key" church administrators, there would be an element of mutual support and respect for higher authority in the crisis decision making process.

The difficulty with the old chain of command was more one of indecisiveness and paralysis in the decision making process. Security events sometimes require immediate answers and all too often, church leaders on every level who generally strive for group consensus may hesitate to make immediate decisions.

Lockdown or evacuation decisions should not be avoided or pondered. Reacting to a disturbance during services should not be micro managed by the pastor or staff, regardless of their capability or training as this oversight creates hesitation, which is time consuming and creates lost opportunity. Robert Greene, in his book, "The 48 Laws of Power," writes, "Hesitation creates gaps."

Plugging into the incident command system (ICS) of outside agencies responding to your church should be a consideration and can add another layer of opportunity to assist responders who may be unfamiliar with your church. Most responding agencies follow FEMA's IC system known as the "National Incident Management System (NIMS)."

NIMS and NIMS training program information is detailed at https://www.fema.gov/national-incident-management-system.

Certification is available at: NIMS online course certificate contact Independent.Study@fema.dhs.gov.

According to the FEMA 100 series incident command structure, an incident command system will consist of and Incident Commander who establishes incident objectives, strategies, and priorities and will assume overall responsibility for the incident.

Four key roles serve under the Incident Commander:
Operations - determines tactics and resources for achieving objectives and directs the tactical response.

Planning - collects and analyzes information, tracks resources, and maintains documentation.

Logistics - provides resources and needed services.

Finance/Administration - accounts for expenditures, claims, and compensation, and procures needed resources.

Our team's ICS would plug into the Logistics Officer in a responding agencies ICS system. We would become a resource and could be used to help in different areas, mainly offering assistance with describing structures, organizing parking lot details, and controlling individuals who may come to pray or gawk at the operations.

Our old SOGs did not succinctly describe the chain of command that would be required to respond to every situation, and therefor was flawed. Making mistakes is a keystone for learning. One of the best ways we can build a foundation and pass our knowledge on to future generations is write down successful ideas and methodologies that helped us succeed. Thus, the old SOG is flawed, and I'm not going to muddy up the waters by reprinting it I this book.

When I started on the team, no one was quite sure who the volunteer security leader was. There was no clear chain of command. In the chain of command, decision making starts with the Team Director.

1. Volunteer security team is administered by the **Executive Pastor**. It is a paid staff position whose reach may encompass all campuses. This person is responsible for all worship team activities. This pastor will also serve to relay information between the church and the security team.

This pastor is the top of the chain at the church. In our situation, it is the pastor our Team Director will report to and be accountable to. However, the pastor is not on the Incident Command list, which starts with the Team Director and works down.

2. **Volunteer Security/EMS Team Director:** Coordinates team leaders and their primary and satellite campus teams. Volunteer

Security Director Worship Security Director is responsible for all planning, coordination, training, compliance, and response of teams. Reports to the executive pastor This position oversees recruiting and retention initiatives, responds to requests for audit information, and communicates with the church regarding Volunteer Security/EMS Team requests. Additionally, this position is responsible for calling a monthly meeting of security team leaders, creating the agenda, and presiding over the event.

Importance of chain of command is for checks and balances. The higher in the chain we go, the more experience and knowledge the leaders should have. In an immediate response to a critical event, we need to establish who is in command, at least for the first five minutes or so until outside agencies begin to arrive and take over.

In any situation where violence is perpetrated or emergency response is needed, it is imperative that your church have a plan that will include stopping the violence, aiding the injured/stopping the bleeding, and recovering from the incident to bring the church back to some semblance of normalcy.

Preplanning for the short term impact on the church and its congregation is essential and should include items like: a designated media person, pastoral help and prayer team response, controlling crime scenes, directing media and their satellite trucks, restricting access, and dealing with post-traumatic stress that will affect many in the congregation.

In the long term, this plan could also address issues like scene cleanups, construction to remove evidence of the incident, and could include memorial planning and commemorations that may extend out for years after the event.

Someone in the chain of command should assume the task of writing these plans and identifying who will be in command. Our incident command system is as follows:

1. VST Director (TD) will serve as Incident Commander until turned

Then in descending order, when the VST Director is not available:

2. VST Assistant Director (AD)
3. VST and EMS Team Leader (TL)
4. VST and EMS Assistant Team Leader (ATL)
5. VST/EMS Team Member

We further define our IC system with the following chain of command sequence:

Should TD, TL, and ATL not be available, the following order will determine the order of incident command and if necessary, incident command: P11, P10, P9, P6, P5, P8, P7, P4, P3, P2, P1.

There is also an understanding that any person serving in the capacity of EMS will oversee and direct the response to any EMS calls.

We've covered defining roles of Team Director, following are defining roles for other positions on our team:

1. **Volunteer Security/EMS Assistant Team Director:** Works directly with the Team Director and substitutes when they are not available. This person should be aware of every aspect of team operations.

2. **Executive Protection Team Leader:** Bigger churches with multiple pastors may want to consider an Executive Protection Team. This may be a separate team providing one-on-one security with an assigned pastor. Their job is much more focused on a personal basis than the typical VST position. They may operate under different guidelines, may extend coverage to all areas of the church campus – which could also include domestic and foreign travel. Their operations are not shared with the Volunteer Security/EMS Team members and will not be discussed in this book. Our security team offers a good breeding ground for potential executive protection team members and our training is a part of their program.

3. **Volunteer Security Team Leader:** Responsibilities include recruiting and retention of team members, training and enforcing SOGs, leading team activities and prioritizing assignments, including assignment of working tasks at any time while security services are being performed. The security leader becomes primary communication with outside agencies and may speak on behalf of the Worship Security Team in the absence of superiors or when asked by church leaders. Manages all team incident reports, training, and team membership. Responsibilities may also include scheduling, training, supply orders, repair orders, and record keeping. Security Team Leaders will work to develop leaders and comprise a Security Team Leadership committee that will meet once per month.

4. **Volunteer Security Team Assistant Leader:** will be appointed by the Security Team Leader and may be replaced at will. This position may take over for security team leader during services and/or complete specific assignments in their absence or upon request. Security Team Assistant Leader may serve as an alternate and may attend Security Team Leader Committee meetings.

In this book, we cover the importance of recruiting and we will get a bit more into leadership. Team members are volunteers and understandably life sometimes gets in the way of volunteering. We need to prepare our teams with leaders who are capable of taking over and running the team.

Some churches have experienced changing security leadership; some have gone through this many times. New leadership comes in, establishes a vision as all good leaders will, and finds difficulty achieving their goals. The biggest problem is, without written SOGs that include purpose, scope, and goals, all we have is a new leader with a vision that cannot be totally shared. They get frustrated, find some place where their talent is accepted and they leave.

I don't know what is worse, the person who leaves the church they love because they feel stifled, or the people doing the stifling because of fear. I wish I didn't have to make that comment, just as I wish security teams didn't have to be a topic in church. This book shouldn't even be necessary.

Continuity between leaders is more successful when written guidelines are in place. This process has been proven to be more effective. And thus, our expectation is that leaders will stay, or at least they won't leave out of frustration. However, people do take short leaves for vacations, illness, work hour changes. Some will move or die. And some will be redirected by the Holy Spirit. There is a long list of events that can happen that may take them out of a leadership position. And so, we ask team leaders to appoint someone from their team who has leadership potential and mentor them. There is always someone who can replace leadership and there is no fear that the team will suddenly stop providing services.

5. **Volunteer Security Team Member:** is a member of the church congregation in good standing, follows SOGs and protocols, attends required training, greets worshippers warmly, always on the alert for people of interest, disrupters, intruders, vandals, etc. Follows the SOGs actions of Deter, Delay, Detect, Deny; respond to and recover from loss events, and assist calling emergency medical services. Communicates all facts to team members. Follows orders of Security Team Leader.

6. **EMS Team Leader:** This position will be held by one EMS team member who will also be responsible for ordering all medical stock and replacement stock, any EMS training for Security Team members, organization of EMS reports, and will be included in the Security Team Leader Committee.

7. **EMS:** The highest certified EMS responder is the leader at any EMS response. Responsibilities include: maintaining EMS certifications through outside sources, following SOGs, alerting team leader when supplies need to be ordered, and battery maintenance of the Automated External Defibrillators (AEDs).

Security team members and EMS may be asked to volunteer at church events such as musicals, etc. Teams may volunteer as a team, but it is not a requirement. Teams will be assembled on the day of the event, a leader will be chosen, and the chain of command will remain in place.

No team member may communicate with outside agencies, speak on behalf of the Volunteer Security/EMS Team, or imply that they speak on behalf of the security team to any person or the media. (See media SOG 3.2)

Your team structure may be different depending on the size of your congregation. Most congregations will not need this type of organization. However, you should have at least one Security Director who can also be a Team Leader. This person may also be the EMS responder and be the link between the team and the church. Identify someone who can establish command and control of an incident that requires outside response.

Also consider having an assistant team leader who will learn the position and lead the team when the team leader is not in attendance. This assures that team standards are met when the leader is not present and will also help future transitions as team members become team leaders.

Team members should have certain expectations of their team. Leadership and the chain of command should be apparent and operate in a hierarchy it is intended for. For example, a new team member has a question and seeks an answer – they should go to their next highest in the chain which would be the team leader or assistant team leader. When they don't get a satisfactory answer, they should be able to address their issue to the next person in the chain. Granted, in a smaller church that chain may be shorter, but we need to look beyond just today and any church that seeks growth should view these protocols as a foundation for the future needs of their security team.

How would it look to the team if the team director went to a team member to discuss problems they were having with pastors. This is how politics start. The intention cannot bring resolution, thus the only real result is building consensus with someone who can be an ally and possibly help apply pressure (use any name here – logic, support, solidarity) on the church. Identifying and implementing a chain of command is a very important step.

Chapter 8

COMMUNICATIONS

On the web site, Fellowshipone.com, William Chadwick wrote, "7 Critical Essentials for Church Security - You were called to be Ambassadors of Peace and Safety."

"Simple two-way radios are the most effective way to share information and coordinate people during emergencies," says Chadwick. "They're better than cell phones that depend on coverage and up-to-date numbers." The emergency response teams should have a clear command structure, knowing who will be responsible for communicating with teams throughout the facility. In large churches, it is important to have specific "zones" identified so that each team knows the specific evacuation plans or, in certain situations, lock-down protocols to keep people safe. - See more at: http://www.fellowshipone.com/resources/church-management/7-essentials-for-church-security#sthash.UC9WBTaQ.dpuf

Proper communications fulfills our goals of detection and response.

VST Communications SOG:

6.1.0 Proper Etiquette for Radio Use
a. Always use an earpiece properly attached to your radio to prevent speakers from being heard.
b. Earpieces may be provided by the church or purchased by VST member.
c. Use of profanity, inappropriate remarks, and outbursts of music is prohibited.
d. Identify yourself by your position, followed by the person you are trying to contact.

6.2.0. Radio Use
1. Radio Use:
   a. Use designated radio channel
      i. VST is channel 1.
      ii. Outside security is channel 2.
      iii. Special events – see posted channel being used by radio chargers.
   b. Know what you want to say before you key the mic.
   c. Make certain you are on the correct channel.
   d. Wait a couple of seconds after keying the mic before speaking.
   e. Keep it short and simple.
   f. Remain calm, speak clearly.
   g. Do not whisper. If necessary, use your hand to shield your voice.
   h. Clear text – plain English should be used for all communications.
   i. Remember – others are listening.

2. In an emergency
   a. State your position.
   b. State 9-1-1 or Emergency.

3. Report any radio or transmission problems to your team leader.

4. Radio communications are for VST essentials and response during services.

5. Radio check upon starting a shift.
    a. Announce check.
    b. Await response and acknowledge.
    c. If no response:
        i. Check that radio is turned on and on the correct channel.
        ii. If radio is on and channel correct, try a new headset.
        iii. If the problem was the headset, take the old headset and set it aside – let your team leader know it didn't work.
    d. If your radio was on and the headset is not the problem – get a different radio, put the old one aside, and inform the team leader.

6. Pre service/event communications
    a. Discussing guest arrival, special needs, construction, detours, etc.
    b. Obtain clarification(s) from team leader.
    c. Relay pertinent information regarding "People of interest" (POI) or "Doesn't look right" (DLR).

7. Assignment confirmation:
    a. Five (5) minutes prior to services team members should be at their assigned posts.
    b. Team leader will request confirmation.
    c. Reply with your name and position assignment.

8. Reporting EMS incident by radio:
    a. Report location, person or people involved, a quick description, and if EMS is needed.
    b. Once on scene, EMS will decide if transport is necessary.
    c. EMS may call for additional supplies or assistance. Roamers and positions 5 and 6 will respond first.

9. Reporting Incidents:
    a. Report position assignment, where you are going, and why.

b. Request backup or backup positions.
c. Relay all known information:
   i. Person(s): gender, height, race, weight, age, clothing, distinguishing features. Vehicle(s): type, manufacturer, color, year, distinguishing features.
   ii. Location: signs of vandalism, break-in, safety concern, any special needs like clean up, person pick up, etc.
   i. Other: Fire, loose animal, lost child, incoherent adult, suspected bomb, etc. Reporting a Person of Interest (POI) or something that doesn't look right (DLR):

10. DLR Person(s). Report:
    a. Gender, height, race, weight, age, clothing, distinguishing features.
    b. Detail why you feel this is someone to watch.
    c. Security leadership may determine that the POI should be denied entry. This call would require backup and an incident report. Obtain as much information as possible.
    d. If not detained, try and find where they are sitting.
    e. If possible, take a picture of the DLR.
       i. Pictures you take, using your personal device, falls under the Social Media policy 3.3.0.

11. Non Person. Report:
    a. Describe what you see and exactly where you are.
    b. Detail why this is important.
    c. Relay emergency response if needed.

12. Reporting any suspicious activity and safety concerns:
    a. People in areas where there should be no activity.
    b. Disruptions.
    c. Vandalism.
    d. Safety concerns.
    e. Emergencies.

6.2.0 Procedure for calling outside agencies.
1. Radio campus police officer or security guard and make your request for outside services.

2. If there is no campus coverage or no immediate answer use your cell phone and dial 9-1-1.
   a. Provide 9-1-1 dispatch with the following:
      i. Location information - Building number and physical reference
      ii. Church address: (Removed by me)

3. Stay on the phone until 9-1-1 releases you.

4. Advise VST team on channel one (1) that an outside agency is responding to your call. VST team leader will advise outside security on channel 2.

5. Outside security will direct responding outside agencies. In their absence, a VST member may be asked to take on this responsibility.

Radio communications we use are quite common and can be purchased "new" for less than two hundred dollars per unit for a top of the line sixteen channel, five watt unit. A good ear piece with microphone could run an additional fifty dollars or so. Less expensive units can be purchased on E-bay and Amazon. Walkie talkies should come with chargers, antennas, and a belt clip.

Review your risk analysis. You will want each team member to have a radio during services. Decide if you also want a pastor or head usher to wear a radio. Any police officer on site should also have access to a radio. I would also suggest at least two or three extra radios for use if one unit goes down or in cases where outside agencies respond and may want a church radio for communications with the team or someone from the church who can help them navigate the property or assist with incident command.

Most security teams I have visited have a cabinet where walkie talkies are kept and recharged. Radios are numbered and team members are asked to list that number next to their name on the sign in sheet. This helps identify radios that need maintenance.

There is also a variety of channel capacity on radios. Earlier in the SOGs "Channel one" was indicated for worship security. At our church, channel two is used for cart drivers and outside security. We actually have the ability to assign sixteen channels. We do have a full list of channel assignments and open channels. The amount of channels your church will need for security is one. Costs may increase with additional channel capabilities, but you'll find multiple channel units are extremely common.

About Two Way Radios:

Choose the right two-way radio. UHF is going to be your best bet in most circumstances for worship security. UHF radios will never be able to communicate with VHF radios. So, if you already have radios and are looking to purchase additional units to use with them, be sure to select the same band. UHF walkie-talkies with a good-sized antenna and enough power will reach further into a building and push through and around steel, concrete, wood and earth. If your two-way radios are going to be used exclusively indoors or if they'll need to go indoors and outdoors, UHF is hands down your best choice.

VHF radios (Very High Frequency) walkie talkies work best when there's a clear line-of-sight between the sender and the receiver with little obstruction. VHF radios are used exclusively in aviation and marine communications where signals are sent across open bodies of water or between the sky and the ground. VHF band walkie-talkies are also great for open fields, golf courses, landscaping and for outdoor security situations with few obstacles. Typically, VHF antennas are longer than those built into UHF radios because they need to facilitate transmission over longer distances and accommodate the VHF frequency range.

Smaller walkie talkies used for sporting and family recreation are closer to being toys than the heavy use radios you are looking for. They're not built to endure the handling and use our teams will put on them. These radios, used on a regular basis for security team purposes will typically break within a relatively short time. Higher end radios, on the other hand, will generally last years with proper maintenance.

Range is another consideration. Realistic ranges for handheld Business Radios vary from 1-4 miles depending on the power capabilities of the unit, weather conditions and obstructions. Basically, the more power (wattage) the radio puts out, the stronger the signal and thus, the more reliable the reception at greater distances.

Two-way radios use between .5 watts to 5 watts of power to broadcast a signal. Better business use radios run between 1 - 5 watts depending on the model. Usually, a higher wattage allows for greater range and is more expensive. Typically, a 1 watt walkie-talkie with an average number of obstructions in its path yields about a mile of coverage. Range increases by approximately 30-50% if you double power. So, a 2 watt walkie-talkie might broadcast within a range of 1.5 miles. 3 watts = 2 miles. 4 watts = 2.5 miles. 5 watts = 3 miles. Actual distances may vary widely based on weather, UHF Vs. VHF, etc. But these are good, general rules of thumb. Four and five watt radios cover still greater distances outdoors and between 350,000 square feet or 30 floors indoors.

Looking to buy a newer model that will work with your older walkie-talkies? Look for a model that uses the same frequencies. If your old radio was pre-programmed with custom frequencies, it probably won't work with other radios, even if you choose the same model. Check out www.techwholesale.com for information on manufacturers and compatibility.

Lower end walkie-talkies might use AA or AAA batteries, but most two-way radios use NiCad, NiMH or Li-Ion batteries. The higher the wattage of your radios, the quicker it will drain power. Certainly, there is enough power to run for a few hours every few days as long as the batteries are charged.

Back to SOGs:

Team members pick up a radio and an ear piece, which is both kept in the same place. Some team members prefer to purchase and retain their own personal ear piece. Just be aware that different radios may require different ear pieces – even between some radios manufactured by the same company.

Ear pieces will usually include a "Push to talk" (PTT) button that activates the microphone. We require team members to perform a quick radio check before leaving the area where the radios are kept, to assure the radio, earpiece, and microphone are working properly. Any equipment that is not working properly should be tagged and taken out of service until a better inspection can be made.

Without earpieces connected, two way radios use a speaker. While the volume can be adjusted, it will be an interruption during services. Additionally, information may be transmitted that should not be shared with anyone other than the security team.

Our inside team uses ear pieces, our outside team does not. One Sunday morning we had just taken up collections and a very large man I had never seen before approached me. This all happened pretty fast, but I remember how he stuck out: About 6'4", 250 lbs., dark complexion, well-groomed beard similar to a Middle Eastern style, wearing a bright yellow and black stripped motorcycle coat and over pants, and carrying a full backpack.

He was obviously upset as he walked right up to me and angrily asked me if I thought he was a terrorist. He demanded to know if I wanted to look inside his backpack. Apparently, as this guy was walking up the sidewalk several outside security guys were standing close enough that the man in the bright bumble bee suit could hear someone calling out, "Check out this guy...he has a backpack and looks like a terrorist."

Although the angry person was de-escalated, the lesson should be to realize that without ear pieces; people will hear what your team is saying.

Some teams may believe cell phones might work better than radios. In certain situations, like higher noise backgrounds, commonly found during worship services – especially for team members standing closer to amplifiers and speakers – team members may have a harder time hearing radio communications. I have heard suggestions that texting via cell phone might be an easier way to communicate. But, there are down sides to using cell phones.

If you have a noisy part of your service, you may want to consider using an ear plug for the ear opposite the earpiece. Some teams use shooting ear muffs when the speakers are too loud. We are in the process of exploring noise reducing gear.

Using a cell phone requires action to retrieve it and turn it on. It forces the user to look down – away from the area of focus, which takes eyes off of a target area. If everyone is included in a group text, it takes everyone's eyes off their focus every time a text is sent. Precious seconds and attention to real-time details are lost. Ringers would be a disruption and vibrations may not be felt. Standing in front of an audience, this process is a distraction and the action of texting during a service may appear disrespectful.

Not that it happens often, but during larger scale incidents, cell phone networks can become overloaded quickly. Dead zones can be experienced in any building or location. Dropped calls occur. Two way radios are the most reliable means of communications for our needs.

Working with a two way radio representative, establish a maintenance plan. Someone on the team should be able to change batteries, antennas, belt clips, and other smaller jobs regarding the radio. They should also be able to clean the plastic tubes on the ear bud end of the earpiece. Instructions will be included with the radios. Also keep a small supply of extra ear tubes, ear buds, and any little plastic connectors that may need to be switched out from time-to-time.

Communication may also include working with Homeland Security, FBI, police, fire, EMS, disaster services, insurance companies and the media. Develop a list of contacts and keep it up to date. Make sure that someone from the church is assigned the task of communicating with these agencies, which could be one person or several people.

One additional link in the communications chain is your churches pastor(s) and anyone who performs counseling. Church staff and volunteers are already directed to report child abuse including: physical, emotional, neglect, and sexual abuse to church leadership. Anyone who counsels should also report any threats or information regarding individuals who may pose a threat to the church to the security team. This information must be kept confidential.

Encompassing many different roles, communications may include many people who should coordinate their efforts to be on the same page. Larger churches may have their security director be the communication lead coordinating church with outside agencies. A different person may be selected to handle insurance and recovery service needs. Another, separate individual may be charged with media communications, and in some instances are actually paid positions for individuals with a lot of public relations experience. This is a strategic role with heavy emphasis on brand management and is responsible for managing all communications, planning activities, and building external relationships with the organization's constituencies, including media. It will be important that all efforts are coordinated and managed.

Chapter 9

ACTIONS

Please notice that up until now everything that has been written is about building a foundation. I've not touched upon actions...but, this is what everyone is wondering about from team members to pastoral staff, directors, insurance company and the church lawyer. George J. Thompson, PH.D, and Jerry B. Jenkins, authors of, "Verbal Judo, The Gentle Art of Persuasion," (2013) write about self-control and the use of, "Verbal Judo" versus "Verbal Karate." The difference being, "judo" uses an opponent's energy and "karate" is more about self-defense. Near the end of the book, they write, "If you can't control yourself, you can't control the situation. It starts with you. You have to be in control to create control."

Our progressive action strategy of Deter, Detect, Delay, and Deny provide guidance for actions by team members. Designed to help our security team remain in control and proactive, rather than be forced to react to someone else and giving up control in an incident.

SOGs Guides: Actions

7.1 Deter
1. Allow your presence to be recognized.
2. Wear your VST identification.
3. Greet attendees with a smile, warm welcome, and handshake.
4. Assure your radio is operational and on.
5. Assure your ear bud is in good working condition.
6. Report to your assigned position and maintain it.
7. Be ready to support another team member in your support zone.
8. Communicate suspicious activity and Persons of Interest (POI).
9. Crowd control is always important; do not allow situations to escalate via the crowd.

7.2 Detect
Dealing with disruptive behavior, such as shouting, cursing or trying to take control of services, must be dealt with quickly and with as little disruption of the service as possible.

1. Be aware. Observe. Always pray with your head up and eyes open.
2. Exercise heightened awareness always. Look for people/events that do not follow base patterns.
3. Respond to church pastors, staff, volunteers and congregants.
4. Communication - Alert the team.

5. The Church will notify VST Team leader of any received electronic, telephonic, written, or verbal threats:
    a. Threats
    b. Staff
    c. Volunteers
    d. People attending worship
    e. Property
    f. Suspicions reports, suspected potential threats
    g. Angry spouse, significant other
    h. Parent custody battle
    i. Restraining orders
    j. Information from other ministries, parking lot, etc.

7.3 Delay

Delay strategies are to slow/disrupt perpetrator's attempts to progress their interruption or to access property and/or specific areas. Physical barriers may be applied, but it is important not to hinder access for emergency responders or routes for evacuation. Security team members may pose as a barrier with back up and team leader approval.

1. Attempt to verbally de-escalate the situation.
    a. Use verbal judo.
    b. Tag out: After 30 seconds, if no success, allow backup to try verbal de-escalation.

2. If unable to immediately de-escalate, instruct the person to go into the hallway for further discussion.

3. Call for police backup.

4. Effective delay tactics allow enough time-between detection and access-for law enforcement officials to respond and catch the intrusion in progress.

5. Concentrate delay efforts away from likely targets in order to keep the intruder from accessing them before help arrives.

6. Ask last question: "Is there anything I can say or do right now that will get you to cooperate with us?"
7. "No" answer – go to Deny.

7.4 Deny
1. The process of denial may be achieved through:
    a. Barriers
    b. Presence
    c. Lock down
    d. Physical denial as a last resort

2. Communicate.

3. Call Police.

4. Back up team members.

5. Perimeter Response – direct incoming government agencies.

6. Deploy VST identification.

7. Assist calling emergency services.

8. Obey all commands of incoming government agencies.

7.5.0 EMS Medical Incident – Procedures
Any VST member responding to an EMS call must always wear gloves where blood or bodily fluids are present. VST EMS only offers basic EMS first response, packaging and stabilization.

1. Radio for help or designate someone else use the radio and call.

2. Do not leave the patient alone to get help or supplies.

3. Stay with the patient until the incident is over.

1. **Decision Matrix**
    a. Can the patient be moved away from the public?
        i. If they have fallen, are complaining of head, neck, back, pelvic, or hip pain do not attempt to move them, except for cardiac arrest, to move them out of the sanctuary before treating if possible.

ii. For all other situations, if the person is ambulatory and they can walk on their own, move them away from the public.
iii. Do not "walk" any person that appears to be in distress. Call for a wheelchair or other walking assistance device.

2. Types of Medical incidents and their treatment
   a. Falls:
      i. If head neck, back, hip, or pelvic pain – consider calling fire department and DO NOT MOVE the patient.
      ii. Cuts and abrasions: Take appropriate actions to stop bleeding, clean and bandage.
      iii. Fractures, broken bones, sprains, and strains – splint or immobilize if possible, apply ice pack, consider calling fire department if unable to splint or needs ambulance for transport.

   b. Diabetics:
      i. Check blood sugar.
      ii. If reading is below 60 or unable to check blood sugar and patient verbalizes they "feel low," give juice and/or food if they are awake and alert enough to eat. If unresponsive, call fire department.

   c. Difficulty Breathing:
      i. Asthma: if mild difficulty breathing and patient thinks their inhaler will handle it, stay with patient and monitor results. If no relief or breathing becomes more difficult – call fire department.
      ii. All other cases – call fire department and give 15 liters oxygen by mask. Keep sitting upright. Do not lie down.

d. Other Medical Problems: i.e. headaches, nausea, vomiting, do not feel well...
      i. Check blood pressure.
      ii. Consider calling fire department if needed or if patient requests it.

3. **Incidents that require Fire Department MUST BE CALLED**
   a. Seizures.
      i. Protect from injury
      ii. Apply oxygen by mask. Flow 15ml.
      iii. Very common for patients to wake confused and resistant. Do not force oxygen if resistant.
   b. Weak or dizzy.
      i. If systolic BP is under 100 – let them lie down and elevate legs if possible.
      ii. Check blood sugar. If below 60, give juice and/or food. Monitor progress.
   c. Unconsciousness (fainting – usually 1 minute or less).
      i. If systolic BP 100 – let them lie down and elevate legs if possible.
      ii. Check blood sugar. If below 60, give juice and/or food. Monitor progress.
   d. Chest pain.
      i. Symptoms include tightness or heaviness in chest, pain radiates to arm, jaw, or neck. Suspect heart issues.
      ii. Keep patient sitting unless they feel like passing out or systolic BP is below 100. Then lie them down.
      iii. Apply oxygen, by mask, at high flow 15ml or 4ml with a nasal cannula.
      iv. Make sure systolic BP is above 120 before allowing a patient to take their own nitro pills.
      v. Keep patient calm and relaxed.

e. Abdominal pain.
   i. Keep in position of comfort, either sitting or lying down.
   ii. Prepare for possible vomiting.

f. Strokes: Symptoms include the following: loss of feeling or movement on one side of the body, facial drooping, slurred speech, unable to speak or confused.
   i. Keep sitting upright if possible.
   ii. Apply oxygen by mask, flow 15ml or 4ml by nasal cannula.
   iii. Check blood sugar.

g. Cardiac arrest
   i. Use continuous chest compression CPR only.
   ii. Do not stop for any reason, until pulse returns.
   iii. Apply oxygen by mask, flow 15ml.
   iv. Have chest compressioners switch off every two (2) minutes for effective compressions.
   v. If trained medical personnel on scene, may bag valve mask respirations – after two (2) minutes of CPR have been completed.

Communications – see 6.2.0

7.6.0 VST Documentation
7.6.1 Security Documentation/Reporting
1. Minor issues that do not require documentation:
   a. POI/DLR alerts
   b. Normal requests from pastors, staff, volunteers, congregants, etc.
   c. Outside security issues where VST is not involved.

2. Reports Requited
   a. All "Delay" events.
   b. All "Deny" events.
   c. Any time "Use of force" is applied.
   d. Anytime outside agencies are called in.
   e. Upon request.

3. Copies of all reports must be provided to the Church Security Director.

7.6.2 EMS Team Documentation/Reporting
Minor issues such as: handing out small bandages or performing blood pressure checks does not require documentation. All other incidents require documentation.

1. Contact Card for minor issues: cuts, abrasions, bumps, bruises, etc., where patient is ambulatory and either patient or legal guardian make decision not to seek additional treatment.

2. Contact Card Information Must Include:
    a. Patient Name.
    b. Name of parent or legal guardian if under 18.
    c. Date of Birth.
    d. Address.
    e. Phone number.
    f. Brief description of the problem and treatment.
    g. Name of EMS team member.

3. Medical Incident Reports must be used for all other types of medical incidents. It will include all the information listed with the contact card and will include the following:
    a. Vital signs.
    b. Recording times of treatments.
    c. Recording time when fire department is called and when they arrive.
    d. An 8 ½ X 11 EMS report must be used.

4. Copies of all reports must be provided to Director of Security.

Here is a fairly decent list of potential incidents and the expected chain of actions our church and team will take. Some things, like tornados and other risks have not been included in this list as our location is Phoenix, Arizona and we have not had a tornado of any significance for decades, we don't get ice or subzero temperatures. Again, this is a guide. For a more accurate plan, you will have to address risks identified on your risk assessment plan.

Incident	Action	Action	Next Action
EMS	Needs Ambulance Need church report	Call 911	Direct responders
Fire/Explosion/ Building Collapse/ Haz Mat	Notify Team Leader	Evacuation Lock down	Implement plan of action
Worship Disrupter	Detect	Delay – call 911	Deny
Civil Disturbances	Detect	Delay – call 911	Deny
Active Shooter / Terrorism	Call 911 Deny	Lock down – Evacuation	Implement plan of action
HVAC/Elevator/ Power failure	Detect	Evacuation/no Evacuation	Call service provider
Flood	Detect	Evacuate	Deter
Demonstrations	Delay - Deny	Call 911 Lock down if threat	Deter
Loss Mitigation/ Recovery	Detect	Call appropriate services	Deter

Every incident will begin a ladder type response. As the event unfolds, your church will climb the ladder towards greater response. This can happen quickly or over time. Please remember that this book is geared only toward protecting the worship service. There are other very vulnerable areas of security like computers, sexual predators, and building design that is not included due to time and space.

The ladder of response starts with your team. As things escalate, the team may call in other resources like EMS, fire and police. This chart is only an example. Also, you will want to determine who the single person is who serve as your communications point person.

Bloodborne Pathogens

Also not discussed, but very important to the safety of your team and your congregation is "Blood Borne Pathogens." We talked about the importance of keeping crime scenes undisturbed, and this topic is equally important. This is as good a place as any for this topic, as we will from time-to-time deal with blood and bloodborne pathogens at incidents.

According to OSHA: Bloodborne pathogens are infectious microorganisms in human blood that can cause disease in humans. These pathogens include, but are not limited to, hepatitis B (HBV), hepatitis C (HCV) and human immunodeficiency virus (HIV). Needlesticks and other sharps-related injuries may expose workers to bloodborne pathogens.

All responders, just like police, fire, and EMS should be trained to watch for bloodborne pathogens and their sources. Security team members may come in contact with an infected congregant, a disrupter who is an IV drug user, or exposed needles in a purse or backpack, someone's pocket, or even one found somewhere on the campus.

The Occupational Safety and Health Administration (OSHA) was created to assure safe and healthful working conditions for employees. Federal OSHA does not generally cover volunteers, unless they are compensated in some way and would therefore be considered employees. Even if Federal OSHA does not cover a volunteer, the state you live in may – always check federal, state, and local laws before instituting a policy. My opinion is, we owe it to our volunteers to make their work as safe as possible.

OSHA does require training for employees who may be exposed to contaminated blood, known as "Bllodborne Pathogen training. Since our security teams may find incidents where they may be exposed to contaminated blood during their service to the church, we have instituted a bloodborne pathogen training. Again, much of what we do is about reducing safety and liability risks.

"In order to reduce or eliminate the hazards of occupational exposure to bloodborne pathogens, an employer must implement an exposure control plan for the worksite with details on employee protection measures. The plan must also describe how an employer will use engineering and work practice controls, personal protective clothing and equipment, employee training, medical surveillance, hepatitis B vaccinations, and other provisions as required by OSHA's Bloodborne Pathogens Standard (29 CFR 1910.1030). Engineering controls are the primary means of eliminating or minimizing employee exposure and include the use of safer medical devices, such as needleless devices, shielded needle devices, and plastic capillary tubes."

Standards that apply to workers may not apply to all volunteers. Individuals and volunteers who may perform "Good Samaritan" acts are not, per se, covered by this standard, although OSHA would encourage an employer to offer follow-up procedures to an employee who experiences an exposure incident as the result of performing a "Good Samaritan" act. This is because such an action does not constitute "occupational exposure", as defined by the standard. Volunteers are not usually covered under OSHA, so technically churches do not have to do anything under this rule, but in keeping with our desire to protect our church, team, and congregants, we do want to educate our team members. See a copy of our Bloodborne Pathogen sheet in the appendix.

Actions

Back to "Actions:" I believe the processes of Deter, Detect, Delay, and Deny are the backbone of our security team. It is a detailed progression that offers team members an orderly guide to help them make determined decisions when appropriate. Throughout this book, we have discussed Deter, Detect, Delay, and Deny – and got into more depth in Chapter One, talking about the seven touches and again in Chapter Four – Protocol. Now, here in this Chapter, it is appropriate to revisit this in a bit more detail.

Sun-tzu, author of, "The Art of War," once said, "To win a hundred victories in a hundred battles is not the highest skill; to subdue the enemy without fighting, that is the highest skill."

To this end, we have created a matrix to be used in training – kind of like a football quarterback wearing a cheat sheet on their forearm to call plays. This matrix offers a quick, simple, understandable step-by-step process for any team member to follow.

I like to compare this process to the Bible. The Old Testament is needed to prove the New Testament. Without the prophecies of the Old Testament, Jews would not have known what prophecies the Messiah would have to achieve to be considered as the messiah. The New Testament proves the Old Testament, because it provides an account of Jesus completing every prophecy.

Imagine, Jesus appearing before prophecy was written or in the Garden of Eden before sin. It wouldn't make sense. If there is no sin, we don't need a Savior and He would not be recognized as such by man. However, we know Jesus Christ is our Lord and Savior, because the Old Testament tells us what that person looks like and the New Testament confirms what He did.

It may be a bad or cheesy analogy, but this book is reaching out to Christians. Missing or rearranging any of the steps outlined in the Deter, Detect, Delay, and Deny guidelines below is like a security strategy that doesn't make sense either.

As we were in the process of onboarding a team from another campus, we talked about Deter, Detect, etc. A very knowledgeable person that was taking through the campus insisted that Detect came before Deter. Not to take that person to task, but if we have a communication problem with the order of our security meme, well…can you imagine what's going to come up in the next steps?

The premise of this book is not to sell you on the fact that you need a security team. Evidence has demonstrated that regardless of whether or not your church has an organized security team or not – people there are performing a security function and your church could still be liable. And, in churches that do have an active security detail – only ten percent of those have any actual operating guidelines or procedures. Again, your church could be liable.

Additionally, this process will offer your church the ability to implant a predictable process that will support the churches mission and goals, deliver a working plan that will give your team a foundation on which to build, provide the best protection for pastors, staff, volunteers, and congregants, and take team member safety into consideration. Tailoring these SOGs to meet your churches needs includes training, where your goal is to make your own matrix and make it second nature. Every team member should have the ability, through practice, to look at a situation and determine where they are on the Deter, Detect, Delay, Deny matrix.

Each step in the process is designed to move up to the next step in a sequential order. The goal is to eliminate any disturbance or threat with the least amount of effort. Skipping any step will result in your team's inability to go back to a reduced effort and could cause things to escalate quicker, which would put more people in danger and at risk of a liability claim.

We can observe an incident going from baseline calm or zero to full blown in a matter of seconds, but we can never put the proverbial "Genie back in the bottle," once we have moved past that point. In other words, we started at Deter and it went to Deny in an instant. Chaos can be crazy, but if we identify this now as, "DENY" – we can act accordingly. However, if we skip, "Detect," or go from "Deter" directly to "Deny," when "Detect" could have prevented an overreaction, or "Delay," would have been a much better option, we cannot walk back our actions and the church as well as the team could be held liable in a civil suit and the safety of other congregants could be jeopardized.

Back in the chapter about teams and team building, I wrote about veteran team members who were unable to accept the new SOGs. One of the basic tenants a few of them couldn't get past was the fact that they were now being asked to wear an identifier pin. This is an important part of the first foundation principle to "Deter." Once that option of deterring is gone, now we have to pray that our ability to "Detect" is right on. We can't go back.

Deter

"Deter" is the act of deterring, which usually means discouraging someone from doing something. One way we deter others is by instilling doubt into their idea of success, which includes a fear of the consequences if they are caught. We make people think twice about their decision to interrupt our lives. And, when successful, we prevent the occurrence from ever happening, which is the desired and most successful result.

According to the U.S. Department of Justice, Office of Justice Programs, National Institute of Justice (NIJ), post, "Five Things About Deterrence, ""Research shows clearly that the chance of being caught is a vastly more effective deterrent than even draconian punishment." And, "police deter crime when they do things that strengthen a criminal's perception of the certainty of being caught. Strategies that use the police as "sentinels," such as hot spots policing, are particularly effective. A criminal's behavior is more likely to be influenced by seeing a police officer with handcuffs and a radio than by a new law increasing penalties."

It's worth mentioning again, that bad people disguise themselves as good guys to get into our good/safe spaces. Those spaces in a church can be separated into three perimeters: outer or parking lot, immediate outside, and the inside sections. When you do your risk assessment, these areas can be defined based on what makes sense for your location, manpower, and risks.

Our church sits on about 72 acres of land that abuts a small mountain, which creates a natural barrier. Generally, unless they're going out for a hike, people aren't climbing over the mountain to get to us. A bad guy trying to act like a good guy will, most likely, come in through the front door along with everyone else.

We should begin to make sure physical deterrents are placed at every opportunity. Physical barriers such as fences, walls, and vehicle barriers act as the outermost layer of security. They may serve to prevent, or at least delay undesired occurrences, and may also act as a psychological deterrent by defining the perimeter of the church and making intrusions seem more difficult.

Security lighting is another effective form of deterrence. Intruders are less likely to enter well-lit areas for fear of being seen. Doors, gates, and other entrances, in particular, should be well lit to allow close observation of people entering and exiting.

According to Keven Marier "Security Magazine, http://www.securitymagazine.com/articles/82833-the-5-d-s-of-outdoor-perimeter-security), March 5, 2012:

"The Deter perimeter is the farthest one from the location of the assets and is often a mix of physical infrastructure such as fences and lighting. The security objective on this perimeter is to deter the criminal from even attempting a breach of the system. Applying surveillance technology along the deter perimeter typically requires the use of overt, large enclosures, which make it obvious to all approaching the perimeter that they are under surveillance." This would include signs that indicate people are under surveillance.

"The detection perimeter's security objective is to monitor large areas of space to accurately detect possible unauthorized intrusion in time to respond appropriately. Surveillance camera technology, especially megapixel cameras, is very effective as an accurate detection tool. Important objectives are the timely notification to security personnel, and having the ability to digitally or optically zoom into the area where intrusion was detected.

Delay actions, "Is typically a security personnel response that attempts to apprehend (or de-escalate) the intruder. Surveillance is used at this perimeter to record the apprehension and determine the effectiveness of the response. "

The outside section is our parking lot. People arriving may see police directing traffic. They see people walking from their cars and greeting others. They'll see our Men's Ministry Team driving carts and standing ready to assist others. Additionally, greeters will be stationed at the front of walkways (seven touches). Vendors and ministry booths may be present. Cameras may be strategically placed and uniformed security guards patrol the outer perimeter. They may or may not see our security team scanning the entrance area, but if they do see them it will be because they are out of the baseline and wearing an identification of some sort.

Is it possible that a potential disturber or threat might think twice about coming in? The only way can really measure this is to compare how many disturbances we had prior to the increased security team, compared to today. "Physical security," is huge industry with certified professionals that focus on these issues.

If there isn't enough to deter this bad person disguised as a good person may now enter your building through a common church entrance. It may sound strange, but this person who is acting like a "nice guy," probably won't come in through an emergency exit or an open window. Remember, they want to appear normal. And now they have to pass more greeters, maybe a pastor who is also greeting, a greeter handing out programs, the desk of our First Impression team, more people, more booths, and more cameras. And again, our security presence is obvious

Going into the sanctuary, they pass ushers, congregants, and see more people watching. There may be more cameras. All along the way, people are welcoming congregants and no matter which rung on the ladder this person is at, not following through on the planned disruption may seem like the better option for the perpetrator.

Our monthly volunteer Security Team training sometimes includes greeters and ushers, especially when we perform awareness training. We teach them, along with our security teams, be aware of people who don't fit the baseline actions of people who typically attend church. No other judgement is needed. Our church is open to all who seek redemption through Jesus Christ and that includes the homeless, addicted, broken, out of work, sick, etc. We accept and encourage all people, regardless of their position to come in and receive God's mercy and grace through His Word. Everyone is welcome. Just don't interrupt the service or pose a threat.

Detect
When those who are intent upon causing harm or interrupting the service are not deterred, we are now charged with trying to detect them before they can achieve their goals. Failure to make eye contact, mumbling or not answering when someone says, "Good morning," carrying a suspicious package, obvious or suspected intoxication, verbal abuse towards volunteers, outright threats, or even if someone just makes the hair on the back of your neck stand up is reason enough for an usher or a greeter to wave to a team member. Suspected individuals are labeled POI – person of interest.

POIs may be watched and may also be approached by security team members. This is where we ask our team to be ready to pray with someone if the opportunity presents itself. Upon greeting the POI, start a conversation. Ask them their name, share yours, and welcome them to church. Ask if they have been there before, if they know anyone, and how they heard about the church. Maybe they have a special need or a question. Observe the replies and actions. Try and assess the person's mood, if they may have a weapon, and other small talk, if possible. It is a lot easier to detect someone who may have bad intentions, than it will be to try and de-escalate them later. This is also adds to the goal of deterring.

We use the Marine Corps Combat Hunter system for detecting potential disrupters. Again, bad people get into our space by acting like good people. Only, they know they are acting and they worry about their missteps, because they know they are not really good people, and they look around to see who is watching them. They look for cameras, security team members, ushers, greeters, and congregants who may be looking at them. Their heads swivel during times when everyone else is focused on what's in front of them. They are obvious and can sometimes be detected. However, this may not work on a person who is under the influence of drugs or alcohol and it may not work on a person who is mentally imbalanced.

When deterring and detecting doesn't stop someone intent on disrupting, the next step is to delay. This starts the de-escalation stage and could present entirely new dynamics to the church, its pastor, congregants, and definitely to security. The obvious goal is to shut down the disturbance quickly and without violence.

Delay
Delaying or deescalating someone who is now officially a "disrupter," is the next step. After someone enters our safe space undeterred, we will eventually detect them either on our terms or theirs. When we miss the opportunity to detect a potential threat, they will eventually make themselves apparent over time. It is at this time that we employ delay techniques meant to de-escalate the interruption.

For the safety of our team members, we instruct them to speak to disrupters at a distance, out of grabbing range. Many times we will find interrupters planting themselves in the middle of a row and in the middle aisle and congregants sitting in the row need to be asked to move out.

At this point, there is no reason to touch the disrupter. Our primary goal is to talk to them and get them to calm down or de-escalate their interruption. Anytime a response from our team is made, we try to support the initial responder with two additional backup people. Backup does not need to be security team members only, and can include ushers, congregants, church employees, our uniformed police officer, etc. Just having a larger number of responders should give some weight to the team members and help to de-escalate the situation.

Since we could find ourselves addressing this person, or several people at the same time in a narrow row, in front of everyone, we control the response by having one person as the main communicator with the disrupter. Rather than have several people yelling or shouting commands and adding to confusion, we give a team member the opportunity to de-escalate the situation and get the disrupter to leave the main sanctuary.

We developed a system we call "Tag-Out". Our first person to talk with the disrupter gets about 30 seconds to try and de-escalate them and get them to voluntarily walk out of the sanctuary. After 30 seconds has passed, another team member may tap on the shoulder of the first person, indicating they are not feeling as if that first person is making any headway and automatically, the second person takes the first person's place and starts again. If the disrupter is not threatening violence, is not under the influence, and seems capable of conducting a reasonable conversation, this procedure can continue until police are called and make a different decision.

If or when interrupters indicate or go from "interrupter" to "safety concern," the team may enter the Deny zone.

The book, "Verbal Judo - The Gentle Art of Persuasion," by George J Thompson, PH.D. and Jerry B. Jenkins is an excellent book that teaches how to engage and deescalate people through empathy.

Always be aware of other potential threats or people who may be part of the current interrupters team. Assume you are being filmed. And again, desire to resolve this in a Christ-like way.

Once away from the congregation, the church and police can decide what they want to do with this person.

So far, since 02/2016 we have not had to use physical force to restrain or stop a disrupter. That is always the last resort. But, just like the Old Testament supports the New Testament and vice versa, we need to have a step in our process that takes us to a physical confrontation. Additionally, we need to set parameters that protect the church, its congregants, and security team members. As a security team, it is also imperative that we maintain control as long as possible, until police show up, if necessary. But under any circumstance, we put protecting the flock as our main objective.

Deny
Denial means to challenge, oppose, reject, rebuff, repulse and pertains to access. We Deny access to pastors, podiums, congregants, staff, volunteers, secure areas, children, computers, etc. Denying access can be achieved through locking doors, putting up barriers, evacuating or locking down a building, and calling in police or other agencies for higher level help. Sometimes, it may mean physically escorting, restraining, or even neutralizing the threat.

We identify this as a "Worst case" scenario, because they evaded our deterrence, which this person (people) probably had no care or intention of recognizing or allowing the deterrence to stop them anyway. They slipped past our detection, because they may not have cared who saw them or when. It's very possible that the person intent on doing harm is a "good" person – not a bad person trying to act like a good person, and so they did not feel threatened by someone exposing them through their potential mistakes. They never even look around to see who might be looking at them. As they begin to climb the ladder toward achieving their goal, which may include doing harm to others, we may have tried to de-escalate or lost the opportunity due to time, but they are not responding the way we need them to respond and now we must "Deny" them access to that which they seek to accomplish. We must force the intruder down the ladder a few notches until the episode is over.

Make sure you are aware of equal or reasonable force laws in your state.

Certainly, reacting to an immediate physical threat should not require much time, other than the few seconds the initial shock of the incident in progress will take to pass as reality and adrenaline kick in. Response must be immediate. At this most imperfect time, training, communication, and confidence must kick in. Once the commotion is started the outcome will rely heavily on muscle memory. Certainly, without training, without SOGs, without a chain of command, without prayer, the outcome may be significantly different. Shepherds that make up your security team may at some time, be asked to give their life and must be willing to take a life when called for. They must also be prepared for physical confrontation – every one of these things is the "actions" we want to avoid as much as possible. But, in the worst case scenario, when it is not possible to avoid or de-escalate the intruder, our teams deserve to be trained to highest level possible.

In the book, "Verbal Judo," the author talks about his, "Structured response." Aware of the signal phrase, eventually, the officer asks the suspect if there is, "Anything I (he) could say or do to get (them) to cooperate?" When the person says, "No," it is an indication to the team that this person is going down physically and immediately. This is not a game and is not to be taken lightly. An "after incident" review can determine if the team member acted as anyone in their position would or should have acted.

Most of our SOGs are foundational procedures that don't leave a lot of room for interpretation. SOG 7.1 – Action allows a lot of decision making based upon the circumstances at hand.

7.2 Use of Force:

Though use of force may never be experienced in your church, there are situations where security team members may be justified in using force. In those cases, controls must be included in the SOGs, reinforced through training, and demanded by leadership. Use of force should never be considered routine.

When the situation is escalating and use of force appears to be imminent, Volunteer Security/EMS Team members who determine the need to use force shall follow the principle that the degree of force employed, in any situation, should only be employed to the extent reasonably necessary.

According to the Free Legal Dictionary, www.legal-dictionary.thefreedictionary.com/Self-Defense:

"Self-Defense," is defined as, "The protection of one's person or property against some injury attempted by another."

"Self-defense is a defense to certain criminal charges as well as to some civil claims. Under both Criminal Law and Tort Law, self-defense is commonly asserted in cases of Homicide, Assault and Battery, and other crimes involving the attempted use of violence against an individual. Statutory and case law governing self-defense is generally the same in tort and criminal law.

A person claiming self-defense must prove at trial that the self-defense was justified. Generally a person may use reasonable force when it appears reasonably necessary to prevent an impending injury. A person using force in self-defense should use only so much force as is required to repel the attack. Nondeadly force can be used to repel either a nondeadly attack or a deadly attack. Deadly Force may be used to fend off an attacker who is using deadly force but may not be used to repel an attacker who is not using deadly force.

In some cases, before using force that is likely to cause death or serious bodily harm to the aggressor, a person who is under attack should attempt to retreat or escape, but only if an exit is reasonably possible. Courts have held, however, that a person is not required to flee from his own home, the fenced ground surrounding the home, his place of business, or his automobile."

In most states, anyone acting as a security team member may not have to "attempt to retreat or escape." Make sure you are training your team correctly and follow the laws of your state.

According to California Civil Jury Instructions (CACI 2016), regarding a business proprietor's liability for the negligent/Intentional/criminal conduct of others (patrons, delivery people, etc.) there are situations where the proprietor has a duty to provide security to protect the safety of patrons.

For the purpose of volunteer church security, since it is reasonable to assume that churches are vulnerable to some sort of violence it may have a duty to protect the safety of their congregants.

I am not a lawyer, but if I was, and I had a client injured in church incident, where the church failed to protect my client…I'd have a field day. So, let's assume this CA duty is extended to churches. It becomes the duty of a security team and its members to take affirmative action to control the wrongful acts of a third party.

It could be argued, while still claiming self-defense, that security teams may be protected against liability in their duty to act, where such conduct may be reasonably anticipated and where reasonable force was used. In this explanation, a church security team member may not have a duty to try and run, like the business person defending their business, and is justified in their decision to stay and protect others.

The "Legal Dictionary," post also includes: "A person who is the initial aggressor in a physical encounter may be able to claim self-defense if the tables turn in the course of the fight. Generally a person who was the aggressor may use nondeadly force if the victim resumes fighting after the original fight ended. If the original aggressor attacked with nondeadly force and was met with deadly force in return, the aggressor may respond with deadly force.

Courts and tribunals have historically accepted self-defense as a defense to a legal action. As a matter of public policy, the physical force or violence associated with self-defense is considered an acceptable response to aggression."

Adhering to SOGs, security team members should exhaust all other reasonable means before resorting to the use of force. In our SOGs, team members have the ability to decide when to initiate force in the "Deny" stage of "Actions." After someone goes undeterred and undetected, we exhaust every reasonable effort to de-escalate the situation. When we are successful, no use of force is necessary. If we are unsuccessful in de-escalation and the threat begins to pose a safety hazard to others, we enter the "Deny" stage.

Using "Step 4" from the book, "Verbal Judo," cited earlier is worth repeating, the authors wrote their final question that will determine if force is needed. Officers learn to recognize this question and know that physical force is going to follow immediately when a negative answer is given. Thompson and Jenkins question is as follows: "Is there anything I can say or do at this time to earn your cooperation?" The question seeks confirmation as to whether or not the person is willing to cooperate at all or not.

Physical force decisions are irreversible. Decisions must be made quickly and under difficult, often unpredictable, and unique circumstances. This is exactly why we are operating directions, "Guides." This model is intended to provide the best guidance and direction possible to security team members.

According to "Wikipedia," "Most states have codified the common law rule that a warrantless arrest may be made by a private person for a felony, misdemeanor or "breach of peace". A breach of peace covers a multitude of crimes in which the Supreme Court has even included a misdemeanor seatbelt violation punishable only by a fine.

California Penal Code section 837 is a good example of this codification: 837. A private person may arrest another: For a public offense committed or attempted in his/her presence. When the person arrested has committed a felony, although not in his or her presence. When a felony has been in fact committed, and he or she has reasonable cause for believing the person arrested to have committed it.

"Public offense" is read similarly as a breach of peace in this case and includes felonies, misdemeanors and infractions. With certain exceptions an arrest must be made. "Holding them until the police get there", is simply a form of arrest. The officer is accepting the arrest and processing the prisoner on behalf of the private person. In no state may an arrest for a misdemeanor be made without the misdemeanor occurring in the presence of the arrestor. In the case of felonies, a private person may make an arrest for a felony occurring outside his presence but the rule is that a felony must have, in fact, been committed. For example, imagine a suspect has been seen on surveillance video vandalizing a building to the extent that the arrestor believes the damage amounts to a felony. If he finds the suspect and makes the arrest but it later turns out that it was misdemeanor damage, the arrestor is liable for false arrest because a felony had not, in fact, been committed.

Because most states have codified their arrest laws, there are many variations. For example, in Pennsylvania, the courts have ruled that a citizen cannot make an arrest for a "summary offense". In North Carolina, there is no de jure "citizens' arrest". Although it is essentially the same, North Carolina law refers to it as a "detention". Other states seem to allow arrests only in cases of felonies but court decisions have ruled more broadly. For example in Virginia, the statute appears to only permit warrantless arrests by officers listed in the Code. However, Virginia courts have upheld warrantless arrests by citizens for misdemeanors.

Use of force - In general, a private person is justified in using non-deadly force upon another if he reasonably believes that: (1) such other person is committing a felony, or a misdemeanor amounting to a breach of the peace; and (2) the force used is necessary to prevent further commission of the offense and to apprehend the offender. The force must be reasonable under the circumstances to restrain the individual arrested. This includes the nature of the offense and the amount of force required to overcome resistance. "

Once a "Citizen's arrest" has been made, the volunteer security team member is responsible for the safety of the arrested person. Police must be summoned immediately, if not already done, and the suspect will be turned over to their custody as immediately upon their arrival.

7.2 Use of Force

1. Team members will use physical force only to prevent injury to himself/herself, or another person or, when necessary, to remove a threat from church property.

2. Police must be called any time a person is restrained or force is used.

3. Only reasonable force necessary to subdue the threat may be used.

4. Security team members may initiate force at any time after de-escalation attempts have failed or at any time after a weapon has been identified or to defend against a physical attack on themselves, pastors, volunteers, or congregants.

5. Use of force applies to:
    a. Physical threats.
    b. Stopping actual physical violence.
    c. Detaining a threat who has been positively identified in a criminal act.
    d. Protecting others against actions that may endanger the health and safety of others nearby.

6. Restraining methods:
    a. May only be used when reasonable belief exists that a person presents an immediate threat.
    b. No force option or restraint may be used that prevents a person from speaking or breathing.

c. Restraints may be removed after it is determined that the person no longer poses a threat or when they voluntarily leave the property.
d. The only authorized restraints are contemporary name brand handcuffs.
e. Leg-irons, ropes, straps, zip ties, or any other device, are not authorized for use.

7. Restraint techniques must immediately be removed:
    a. When at any time, a restrained person demonstrates signs of distress.
    b. EMS must be called.
    c. Every effort must be made to ensure the safety of anyone being restrained.

8. Justification – physical force
    a. Security team members may use physical force if and to the extent that a reasonable person would believe it necessary to maintain order, but such person may use deadly physical force only if reasonably necessary to prevent death or serious physical injury.
    b. A person acting under a reasonable belief that another person is about to commit suicide or to inflict serious physical injury upon himself may use physical force upon that person to the extent reasonably necessary to thwart the result.
    c. Any other person, who renders emergency care at the scene of an emergency occurrence, may use reasonable physical force for the purpose of administering a recognized and lawful form of treatment and/or stabilization.
    d. Reasonably believing a team member cannot safely withdraw from the encounter.
    e. Protecting a third person.
    f. Protecting against a crime in progress.

9. Justification – deadly force
    a. A person is justified in threatening or using deadly physical force against a threat or disrupter:
        i. If such person was threatening or using physical force against another.

ii. To the degree a reasonable person would believe that deadly physical force is immediately necessary to protect himself against the other's use or attempted use of unlawful deadly physical force.
iii. Team members have no duty to retreat before threatening or using deadly physical force.
iv. Defense of a third person.
v. Protecting against a crime in progress, where deadly physical force is necessary to stop a crime in progress, such as arson, 1st or 2nd degree burglary, kidnapping, manslaughter, second or first degree murder, sexual conduct with a minor, sexual assault, child molestation, armed robbery, or aggravated assault that threatens the lives of others.

10. Reporting
    a. Immediately report use of force incidents to the Team Leader.
    b. Make reasonable efforts to obtain as much information about the threat including:
        i. Name
        ii. Address
        iii. Contact information
        iv. Try and get a photograph
        v. Team members who decide to use physical force must document why they determined this action was necessary. Include any statements, weapons, sudden moves, personal feelings, actual occurrences (including the statements and information of witnesses) that caused you to believe that physical force was needed.
        vi. Indicate any obvious injuries to all parties involved, including pains.
        vii. Get detailed information about police, fire, EMS, and other responders, including congregants who may have helped security team members.

Chapter 10

FIREARMS

Update: This SOG has been removed from our SOGs as per insurance company requirements. It is left in the book, because having a firearms policy is a good tool to control those team members who would carry a firearm. I was told that our insurance company would only allow this standard operating guideline if it restricted firearms to current and retired law enforcement and military. At this time, this is an ongoing concern currently an important issue we are discussing.

While some churches are blessed to have off-duty and/or retired law enforcement officers, and current or prior military people as volunteer security team members, we are blessed to have many shepherds who do not have this experience.

Then again, I question the ability of the seventy+ year old cop that's been retired from the department for fifteen or more years, who hasn't qualified since leaving the department, and who now suffers from arthritis, vision problems, or some other old age related ailment that could impair their ability to respond.

Once the church gives up the right to regulate firearms through SOGs, it gives up control. Understandably, churches don't want to have an incident where a security team member claims to have a right to carry or worse yet, claim that the church gave them permission to carry or knew about them carrying a firearm – especially if something stupid occurred. Your policy could be as easy as – "Volunteers are not allowed to carry firearms." But, in cases where no policy is written, the church may still be liable for individuals who volunteer for security, even though there is no written SOG.

Daniel Blevens wrote a quick book titled, "The Armed Discussion in Your Church." In his thirty eight page book, Mr. Blevens writes what in my opinion is a very succinct discussion about armed security. He, like every other security director or team leader I have ever talked to about this issue stress training and qualifying.

For us, this topic has been one of our greatest challenges. Our state is a Constitutional carry state, meaning anyone eligible to own a firearm can carry it concealed or in the open without a permit. Restrictions are very few and permits are available, but not necessary.

Our church has a policy for employees regarding firearms on the campus. There is no policy regarding volunteers. There is also no policy regarding congregants who carry firearms. This guideline is meant to apply to the VST only.

Security is about controlling unknowns as best we can. When it comes to weapons, what is unknown is who is carrying, what their intention is, how much training and experience do they have, and what risks are they likely to take?

Before implementing any firearms policy, please check with your insurance carrier and legal team. Make sure your church security team is following all local, state, and federal laws.

8.1: Firearms

Any Church Volunteer Security Team member may conceal carry while performing security ministry services to the church as long as they meet mandatory team membership, training, and equipment requirements.

Team membership (see 1.1 Team Membership for details): Any team member who desires to carry a firearm while acting as a member of this team must be a member in good standing and comply with all team member requirements.

Training (see 2.1 Training): Training requirements as per 2.1 must be met, and additional firearm training requirements must be completed.

1. Requirements to Carry
    a. Must submit some form of firearms safety training.
    b. Must comply with all applicable Arizona or state statutes.
    c. Must participate in, and pass all firearms qualification courses, annually.
        - Shoot don't shoot training
        - Combat firearm training
        - Range training and target qualification

Any sworn, certified, peace officer in the State of Arizona or an active federal government law enforcement officer may be exempt from these requirements.

2. Procedures
    a. Firearms must be concealed at all times.
    b. No team member will unnecessarily draw, display or carelessly handle a firearm.
    c. All team members will immediately comply with all police orders.
    d. No team member may fire any warning shots.
    e. No team member may draw their weapon as a threat or use it to try and de-escalate a situation.
    f. Discharging a firearm is only appropriate to stop a life threatening threat.
    g. Always treat your firearm as if it is loaded and the safety is off
    h. Be sure of your target and what is beyond it

    i. Always keep your finger off the trigger until ready to fire

3. Equipment
    a. Approved firearms are handguns with the following calibers: .380, 9mm, .38, .357, .40, and .45. Rifles, all other calibers, and other projectiles are prohibited.
    b. Ammunition may only be hollow point ammunition.
    c. Ball, armor piercing, and hand loaded ammunition is not allowed.
    d. All firearms must be secured in a concealed holster at all times.
    e. Carrying an unapproved weapon is grounds for immediate termination from the team.

4. Other weapons
   It will be acceptable for Volunteer Security Team members to carry certain self-defense weapons such as:
   - Pepper spray or mace
   - Tactical pen
   - Extending baton
   - Stun gun or Taser
   - Tactical flashlight
   - Knife

5. Weapons not allowed
   - Nun chucks
   - Swords
   - Anything that cannot be concealed.

These SOGs should be easy enough to follow. Notice that these are distinguished as "policy" and not "guides." Making the decision to allow weapons to be carried by your security team should be a very cautious decision making process.

According to Mennonite Mutual, in a paper titled, "Guns in Churches Addressing Church Security Needs" July, 2013 (http://www.mennonitemutual.com/wp-content/uploads/2013/11/Guns-In-Churches-Addressing-Church-Security-Needs-201307.pdf) they offer four possibilities for churches to follow.

"Option #1: Never allow guns on church property.

They cite several reasons a church may adopt this policy:
- Support belief that churches are to love their enemies, show the way of peace and be an example of non-violent resolution to conflicts.
- Having weapons brings enormous liability to the church.
- Potential for accidents
- Unintentional injury to innocent bystanders
- Possible excessive use of force
- And confusion when police arrive over who is a threat

All these "reasons" are also downsides that may offset any benefits of additional security.

Option #2: Hire only trained professionals:
- Professionally trained and equipped security agencies or off-duty law enforcement officers.

This choice could shift liability away from the church. Professionally trained security officers and off-duty officers may also be trained in such areas as crisis intervention, de-escalation, and proper non-lethal tactics. Some churches utilize uniformed security personnel, plain clothes security. We use both.

The downside of hiring outside security can be the cost, as well as the concern that the hired officer is not connected to your church and therefore may not represent the church like a member would. They may not have the "servant's heart" when dealing with issues. Also, as we have discussed through this book, whether you acknowledge it or not, your church most likely already had people acting in the "security" role. Hiring outside security as an only option may not bring the desired planning, communication, and relief from liability you seek.

Option #3: An in-house, volunteer, trained security team.

This is the option this book is written for. I have had the opportunity to meet with many teams and see their organization. Team sizes vary. Some churches will have one service a week; others may have six or more. Some are comprised of current and retired law enforcement officers; some are people just trying to be the shepherd. It can be more cost effective to utilize church members who approach issues with a servant's heart that fulfills church missions and vision, and should present a lower key security presence as visitors and congregants may be distracted by uniformed guards or high profile images. It may also be easier to observe and get closer to people without incident using church members instead of uniformed security guards.

Downsides here are accountability and training, but a committed team can overcome much of that.

Bottom line, your church will follow federal, state, and local laws. If firearms are permitted, you will have to make the decision to allow your security team to carry firearms or not. It is not a decision to be taken lightly. It is the reason we have incorporated so much training in our SOGs.

Regarding your decision to allow your security team to be armed - arguments pro and con exist on both sides, just as they do in the public arena today. My point of view is definitely biased. I see the security team as being more than just another ministry. We look for people who are dedicated, professional in their actions, and who accept their role to protect everyone from danger. As I have written many times over, they have to be willing to give their life and be willing to take a life. We refer to our team as a threat assessment and first response team. I believe a security team member who qualifies, should have the ability to protect themselves and their church with every available tool, including firearms.

Maybe your church doesn't have people who can be trusted. I'm not being funny, I understand that we don't necessarily get to pick the people we assign to certain duties and maybe you don't have a person you trust implicitly to have a weapon in church. Or, maybe you support gun control - I would never advocate anyone go against their beliefs. And there are always other options.

Regardless of your policy, always check with your insurance company and church legal advisor. Weapons must be clean and in good working order. Safety must be a top priority.

Chapter 11

EVACUATION/LOCKDOWN

7.1 Evacuation & Lockdown Procedures

911 personnel, VST, or emergency coordinators may instruct that the congregation is to evacuate or to remain in place depending on the type of emergency. Evacuation procedures may vary depending on the nature of the emergency. Buildings will be evacuated when an alarm sounds or upon notification by emergency personnel. Be prepared to do the following:

Evacuation is the orderly movement of people and crowds to a safe zone.
- See "Evacuation Chart in Appendix "D" for zone information and pre-planned designated meeting areas. (Appendix "D" is a reference from our SOGs specific to our church and is not included in the book. You will want to have your own "Evacuation Chart" as an appendix to your SOGs)
- See "Evacuation Routes" in Appendix "D" for evacuation routes.

Lockdown means securing people and crowds in place.
- See "Lockdown Procedures" in Appendix "D."

Know your role in an evacuation/lockdown. Be familiar with evacuation/lockdown procedures from every position.
- Ushers to assist with special needs evacuation.
- In prolonged lockdown situations, Ushers obtain medical needs information.
- Activate the building's alarm if emergency personnel tell you to do so, or if it is apparent that people will be harmed if they do not leave (i.e. fire).
- Stay Calm.
- Help the crowd stay calm using the church communications equipment.
- In an evacuation, communicate evacuation routes and safe zone information.
- Instruct people that once outside, leave the immediate area, or go to a safe zone for further instructions.
- Do not allow people to return to the evacuated area until advised that it is safe to do so by emergency personnel.

Some emergencies may require that you take shelter inside buildings. Incidents such as a hostile person, severe weather or a hazardous material release are examples of times when you may be asked to stay in a specific area.

Public Safety & Security or law enforcement and emergency personnel will instruct you to evacuate or remain in place depending on the nature and context of the emergency. Do not sound any alarm in a lockdown situation.

If you are ordered to lock down an area:
- Go to the closest building.
- Close windows and doors and stay away from them.
- Lock and barricade doors if possible.
- Turn off air-conditioning, ventilation and lighting if possible.
- Close window coverings.
- Remain quiet and in place until notified by emergency personnel.

- Silence phones and do not use them unless you are calling emergency personnel
- In the main church, secure locking doors, stay away from windows in the stairways.
- Once doors are secure, they may not be opened without a police officer present.
- Have congregants fill out a "Get Connected Card," and list anyone who is missing from their group.

Determining the difference between ordering an evacuation and a lock down will depend on where and what the threat is and where the congregation would be safest. Fire moves and consumes oxygen. Congregants are safer away from anywhere the fire could spread and an evacuation is most often the best action. Conversely, a hazardous materials spill or release outside the church could pose certain dangers for congregants if they are exposed to the materials. A lockdown where doors and windows are shut, air conditioners and fans are stopped, and openings in the building can be sealed would be the best option.

In the event of a lockdown alert - Immediately lock the entry door and turn off the lights. Keep congregants inside, away from windows and take cover if possible. If the threat is in your immediate area DO NOT lock the aggressor in your area with you. If you are out in a common area seek the nearest secure shelter (i.e. a nearby classroom, office, bathroom, etc.) If you are in or near the parking lot seek shelter in your vehicle and lock the doors. DO NOT leave the campus. Await contact by police personnel.

Remain in your secured area until further instructions are provided. This may take some time and will require patience. As police pass through the area to investigate and secure the threat, it is also important that you indicate (if possible) to the police non-verbally that your area is secure and the offender is not in that area. This will be accomplished by giving the police a "thumbs up" as they approach your door. If the threat is in your area do not respond to the police. This will signal that there is a potential threat in your area and they will enter the room. If there is no threat in your area the police will move to the next area. REMAIN IN LOCKDOWN!

Once the threat has been contained a police officer accompanied by a church representative will move from area to area to release people from the lockdown. Wait for the official release. This will take some time. Please remain in your area as it will be imperative to provide medical assistance if necessary and the police and/or security may need additional information from you regarding the incident.

Set up Command Center
- Security office in main church or any office in any other building where permitted. Communicate with outside agencies exactly where our Command Center is located.
- Provide VST communications with outside agencies.
   o Use channel 1, unless otherwise instructed.
- Copy of building blueprints kept in VST office.
- VST ICS plugs into outside agency ICS.

Once an evacuation has been started, ushers should assist disabled persons. If you encounter smoke, take short breaths through your nose and crawl along the floor to the nearest exit. Feel all doors with your hand before opening, heat will be easy to detect, because the door will be hot. If the door is hot, do not open it. If the door is cool, open it slowly, keeping behind the door in case you have to quickly close it to protect yourself from oncoming smoke or fire.

Proceed to the ground level and outdoors. Move upwind of the building at least 75 feet away from the building and beyond designated fire lanes. Do not go to your automobile or attempt to move it from the parking lot as this could hinder access by emergency vehicles. Do not congregate near building exits, driveways, or roadways. Do not re-enter the building until an "all clear" is issued by the incident coordinator or the fire department. Do not allow others to reenter. If someone is missing, obtain information and call it in to the command center.

Active Shooter Response

Warning Signs If you have had contact with ANY individual(s) who displays the following tendencies, notify the team and the officer on premises, if one is available. If no officer is on premises, contact law enforcement when you observe any of the following:

- Threatens harm or talks about killing others.
- Constantly starts or participates in fights.
- Loses temper/self-control easily.
- Possesses or draws artwork that depicts graphic images of death or violence.
- Becomes frustrated easily/ converts frustration into uncontrollable physical violence.

When a hostile person(s) is actively causing deadly harm or the imminent threat of deadly harm or is barricaded within a building, the following procedures should be followed:

Run:
- If you are on the security and you are unarmed, run if you can do it safely.
- Use any means of escape: doors, windows, etc.
- Guide others to escape.
- Find a safe place outside, warn others not to go inside, assist police by providing as much information as you can.

Hide:
- Lock yourself in the room you are in at the time of the threatening activity.
- Do not stay visible in open areas. In a larger room, hide under furniture or other fixtures.
- Lock windows and close blinds or curtains.
- Turn off all lights and audio equipment.
- Stay quiet and calm.
- Do not sound the fire alarm as it will alert the threat that people are still in the building.
- If communication is available, call 911.
- First in officers will not be searching for you until all threats are neutralized. Even if you are injured, police will not be there to help you.
- EMS will not enter until the facility is safe.
- Do not respond to anyone not in a police uniform.

Play Dead
- If you are unable to hide and there are other victims around you, you may choose to play dead.

- Again, be silent.
- Do not turn off your phone – and DO NOT ANSWER your phone when it rings. As soon as information about the incident hits the news, people will try to call you. Victim's phones will also be ringing, so the threat will think it's normal.
- Do not move to help others until you are sure the threat is gone.

Surrender -No Fight
- If you decide not to fight and you can't run or hide, and if the intruder catches you, follow their directions.
- Do not make eye contact.
- Try and stay calm.

Fight
- Fight the intruder.
- Anything can be used as a weapon. Fire extinguishers can be very useful.
- Fight alone or gather others.

Swarm
- Work as a team to disrupt and confuse shooters, opening up a split second to take them down.

Once law enforcement arrives, obey all commands. You may be handcuffed or made to put your hands in the air. This is done for safety reasons, and once circumstances are evaluated by law enforcement, they will give you further directions to follow.

Typically, Emergency Action Plans do not cover every possible situation that might occur. Rather, it should be used as a training tool that can reduce the number of injuries or death if put into action as soon as a situation develops. Time is a critical factor in the management of a situation of this manner.

Keep emergency contact information available and in plain sight:

Evacuation/Lockdown | 169

EMERGENCY TELEPHONE NUMBERS & INFORMATION
For All Emergencies Dial 9-1-1

- If your community is not served by 9-1-1, call your local emergency contact number.

- Caller Name: _____

- Call Back Number: _____

- Church Name: _____

- Church Location: _____

- Closest Intersection: _____

- OTHER IMPORTANT NUMBERS (Provide names and contact numbers for both daytime/business hours as well as night time /24 hr emergency contact)

- Building Maintenance/Trustees/Key Holders: _____
  _____
  _____

- Pastor/Minister(s): _____
  _____
  _____

- Building Coordinator: _____

- Security Director: _____

- Security Team: (Roster)_____

- Medical Response Team Members (Roster) _____

- Other Emergency Contacts:_____

In the event you receive a threat call (i.e. bomb threat, armed assault, custody issues), remain calm; if possible, have a pre-arranged signal to alert other personnel to listen to the caller also. If possible, advise the caller that the detonation of a bomb could maim or injure innocent people.

From the Missouri Faith Based Homeland Security Initiative:

Threat Checklist - Complete this list if you receive a threat.

Exact time of call: _____ Date: _____

Exact words of caller:

_____

_____

_____

_____

_____

Caller's voice: (circle) Male - Female / Adult - Youth

Estimate Age: _____

Black White Hispanic Asian Other: _____

Describe voice (circle all that apply): Calm - Disguised - Nasal Rapid - Accent - Nervous - Angry – Sincere - Slurred - Loud Excited - Giggling - Stressed - Crying

If voice is familiar, whose did it sound like? _____

Background Noise: (circle) Music Children Typing Airplanes Machinery Cars/Trucks Other: _____

Do not hang up! Obtain as much information as possible:

- When is the bomb going to explode? _____
- Where is the bomb? _____
- What does it look like? _____
- What kind of bomb is it? _____
- Method of activation: mechanical, clock, movement/chemical action? _____
- Method of deactivation? _____
- Did you place the bomb? _____
- Why? _____
- Where are you calling from? _____
- What is your address? _____
- What is your name? _____

Call received by: _____ Department: _____
Ext: _____

Note: In the event you receive a bomb threat:
- Call 911 immediately.
- Provide the following information: Identify yourself - State: "I have received a bomb threat." Give your office location and extension.
- REMAIN CALM!

Chapter 12

TEAM LEADERSHIP

So, now you have a set of operating guidelines based on your church's specific risks. You've started recruiting, performing background checks, training, keeping records, and applying the Deter, Detect, Delay, Deny protocols. Leadership is required to assure this system retains its integrity, to continually evaluate the team, assure communications with team members and the church, to establish ties with local police and fire departments, and to review risks and procedures.

Leaders must continually be developing potential leaders. If the program is to succeed, it must be based on a desire for excellence, which is as simple as making excellence an expectation by leaders. Success breeds success. Leaders are accountable to the church and should always be recruiting and grooming others for leadership.

There are a lot of books, CDs, training seminars, and whole lot of information available on the World Wide Web regarding leadership, team management, and motivation. While some suggest that people are either born leaders or are born followers, most will agree that leaders rise when called upon. They don't quit when things get tough. They are dedicated to successfully guiding their teams to meet church and team goals according to their purpose, scope, and goals. There is a litany of Biblical versus regarding leadership and leaders:

Philippians 2:3 – "Do nothing from selfishness or empty conceit, but with humility of mind regard one another as more important than yourselves."

Luke 6:31 – "Treat others the same way you want them to treat you."

Proverbs 11:14 – "Where there is no guidance the people fall, But in abundance of counselors there is victory.

Proverbs 16:12 – "It is an abomination for kings to commit wicked acts, for a throne is established on righteousness."

Exodus 18:21 – "Furthermore, you shall select out of all the people able men who fear God, men of truth, those who hate dishonest gain; and you shall place these over them as leaders of thousands, of hundreds, of fifties and of tens."

1 Corinthians 12:12-31 – "For even as the body is one and yet has many members, and all the members of the body, though they are many, are one body, so also is Christ. For by one Spirit we were all baptized into one body, whether Jews or Greeks, whether slaves or free, and we were all made to drink of one Spirit. For the body is not one member, but many."

Good leaders know about character and integrity. Leaders with integrity know the difference between right and wrong, and leaders with good character are always doing the right thing. There can be no favorites or political gain. All glory goes to God. All works for God's Kingdom. Understanding that it takes a specific type of person who is willing to put in the time, the training, the commitment and the knowledge that at some moment, they may be asked to take a life or give their own – this ministry is not for everyone. Finding and recruiting the right people is key.

Leaders must understand the mechanics of their responsibility and be familiar with the tools available to them. Always striving for excellence, they should always be looking for a better way – not necessarily the easiest or least expensive option, but the best option their budget can afford that provides the highest level of customer service/congregant care combined with the highest level of safety for their team. This includes assuring compliance with the law and takes into consideration liability and insurance concerns.

SOGs provide the continuity and guidance necessary for successful transition from team member to team leader. Our first two team leaders had been on the team for many years and had been exposed to our SOGs. In training, "Actions" were discussed based upon our written guidelines, which offer a predictable line of actions that everyone knows and expects.

When it came time to promote the third team member to team leader, things were quite a bit different. He had not been exposed to SOGs, and if you recall, we were restricted from training SOGs. He had no guidelines and was unaware of our predictable actions training. Since he didn't have a basic structure, it was apparent by the expressions on his face that scenarios were playing through his head and it was hard to grasp what command role he would play. I remember that happening to me when I was first asked to serve as Extrication Officer for the fire department and I rolled up in the BRT (Big Red Truck) to see car flipped in a ditch with power lines lying on the car.

Leaders and potential leaders need to have a plan they can follow. It is one key component of assuring the future of the team. Remember that SOGs can always be altered to reflect new processes according to changing risk assessments, church needs, and new developments in best practices.

Continuing education is equally important. Team leaders should be engaged in the security community. They should understand and find value in communicating with other churches, local and federal agencies, and with organizations who help organize and train church security groups.

When leaders are motivated by outside training, the team should be motivated to follow. In our quest for excellence, as we praise God through our service, we should always be looking for best practices. SOGs should change to reflect these improved processes.

Most important, leaders teach everyone on the team through their actions and communications. Encouraging team members to provide input is a great way to get them thinking and learning the responsibilities of the leadership role.

When I first started firefighting I was like a child in a toy store – all the tools, gadgets, buttons, lights, etc. on the BRT. Trucks were all so big and had so many compartments. It was hard to imagine how anyone could know what every tool was used for and which compartment it was stored in.

Over time, through training, practice, and implementation I did learn about all the tools, their specific use, and where they were located. The trucks got smaller and soon I knew which tool was need where and when without a veteran having to say anything. Our security team is exactly the same way.

My favorite tools were the hydraulic Jaws of Life, cutters, and spreaders. I loved tearing apart vehicles and became very proficient at it. Eventually our department started an extrication competition team and in the second year, I became the team leader.

In our first regional competition, we achieved our goal of getting the dummy out of the crushed car in less than the twenty minute time limit. Our overall score was dinged because, as the extrication team leader, I was not identifiable, because I dressed the same as my team. We also left a tool in the working area immediately surrounding the crashed vehicle, which could be a hazard to team members and the patient. One team member was cited for improper tool usage. These were all small issues that when improved, take us from good to great. And, when transferred to others in our department, allowed our department to offer better services to the community and greater safety considerations to protect the team members. Do not fear making mistakes or criticism. Just try and make those mistakes in training and encourage critiques as part of the learning process.

Our team demanded excellence, not only because we wanted to win competitions, but also because we realized that increasing team competency would translate to increasing department competency and the ability to offer our community a much higher level of service. At the time we started, the average time for an automobile extrication nationally was forty five minutes to an hour. Our goal was to reduce that time to 20 minutes or less.

Identifying the "mechanics" includes understanding the relationship of what you are doing versus what you want to accomplish. With extrication, it was more than just unwrapping or untangling a patient from metal. The goal is based upon the EMS objective of providing the highest level of care by getting patients to the emergency room within one hour of the incident – known as the "Golden Hour."

Obviously, if extrication can take an hour, after it took ten minutes for the fire department to arrive on scene, and an additional ambulance drive of ten minutes, we are well beyond the desired "Golden Hour."

Our team took on the goal of excellence, because that is what leadership expected. Soon, we had firefighters and EMS personnel trying out for team positions. I mean, we had to come up with ways to weed out those who were less dedicated – not that that's an easy task when everyone is committed, faithful, and enthusiastic. Eventually, we had to whittle the group down to seven for competition, but everyone wanted to train, which sparked other firefighters and EMS to want to train and see what all the excitement was about.

People who did not make the team continued to show up for training that went on for months before the competition. Our team cut up about one hundred fifty cars a year just training. Hence, the department and the community benefitted from larger groups learning advanced techniques for extrication and patient care.

I am confident that our team could get any patient(s) out of a mangled vehicle in 20 minutes or less. That leaves plenty of time for stabilization and transport in the "Golden Hour." We took our training, demanded excellence, held each other accountable, and saved more lives.

One of my favorite extrication stories was of a single vehicle roll over on a two lane highway just outside of the city. A handicapped driver in a wheelchair hit a patch of ice and lost control of his van. There was one other passenger. Both were unconscious when the first officer arrived.

The van was resting on its side where the side sliding door was and access through the back was hampered by a five foot drop on the shoulder and the van sticking out about a foot over that. It was cold and icy. The fire department officer was on the radio calling for extrication along with a medical helicopter and he estimated the extrication to take over an hour due to road conditions, the location of the driver (now in the back of the van with his wheelchair on top of him), and the position of the van.

It took us about seven minutes to arrive on scene. We performed a "walk around," of the van that took all of ninety seconds. All the training, preparation, practical experience, research for better strategies and best practices came into play and we had both people out of the van and packaged in ambulances in less than 5 minutes.

During the walk around, almost every team member is expected to be engaged as per our standard operating guides. They must know their position and what the expectations are before the emergency response occurs. They must be familiar with tools and practices. Most important, they must be able to complete the walk around process in 90 seconds or less.

During the walk around, we're looking for hazards like loaded bumpers, downed power lines, chemical spills, unstable conditions, gas leaks, and obstacles. We look at potential points of entry, and we assess the number and condition of people in the car. We also search for ejected passengers or pedestrians that may have been involved. Our goal is to come up with a plan of action for the stabilization and extrication.

Before anyone can touch the vehicle, we need to establish that the scene is safe. So, everyone gets together as a group and we have an open discussion. Everyone is encouraged to verbalize their opinions and ideas. Everyone has input. This is an amazing opportunity to learn how leadership works.

Again…preplanned, heavily trained SOGs. Everyone, all volunteers, assigned a position and doing their assigned job. Just like our volunteer church security/EMS team.

Leaders must have vision, but they must also be open to listening to others ideas and must have the capability of making a decision that does not include ego. Hence, if a team member offers a better idea, the leader should be able to see it and either be able to incorporate a change or explain why they didn't – later.

Primary plans are just that, the first plans. Knowing the goals, tools, procedures, etc. allows us to implement those plans and measure for success. When things are not going as planned, the leader must have options that include changing people, tools, and procedures. Discussing these changes openly, at a team meeting sometime after the incident, allows less experienced team members the ability to understand the team leader decision making process – breeding new future leaders.

The greatest takeaway for me from the extrication competition experience has been this: As a leader, I arrive with my team and immediately see what everyone else sees. I must develop a plan of action based upon our SOGs that everyone understands and expects, because we trained on them. When I communicate with my team everyone knows to expect. This is especially important when the scene is filled with chaos.

I have to be honest and quickly admit anything I am not sure of and I must be able to rely on my team to fill in the blanks.

Every team member is encouraged to offer input at one specific time. As the team leader, I have the authority and trust of my team that their safety and our excellent service to the patient, community, and department (church) are always on my mind. I will seek input, but if the team member is not able to paint a picture of what their suggestion is, or if I believe that my assessment is more correct, I will not change my original plan. However, I will always retain suggestions and keep them on my options list. This allows us to react quicker when and if primary plans fail.

When and if a major incident would happen at your church, everyone and everything will be better protected when your team has taken security seriously and has prepared for the event. When a team is prepared, the actual event doesn't matter. No two events or circumstances are exactly the same. People will need to improvise, adapt, and overcome – and the best way to achieve this is through operational knowledge.

Utilizing team suggestions in training sessions can be fun and insightful. Training is the only place where we want to make mistakes so that teams can learn how they continue to operate when tactics or strategies don't go as planned. Making mistakes in training is good. Making mistakes on scene is acceptable, as long as the team knows how to correct them quickly.

Team leadership is a huge focus in many books, CDs, training programs, seminars, etc. To become a better leader, especially where volunteers are concerned, you should take it upon yourself to include this in your personal education.

Courageous Leadership: Field-Tested Strategy For The 360° Leader, by Bill Hybels (2009 Zondervan, Grand Rapids, MI) includes a chapter titled, "Developing Emerging Leaders." This is the best way a team will grow and give assurance that a volunteer security team will thrive in the future. He writes, "Leaders are at their best when they are performing the functions of leadership – casting God honoring visions, building teams, setting goals, solving problems, and raising resources. When they are modeling exemplary leadership, that's when leaders shine."

He goes on with, "Leaders must exhibit character. When leaders manifest traits like trustworthiness, fairmindedness, humility, servanthood, and endurance over a long period of time, and when they prove themselves to be unwavering in crisis, that is when leaders are at their best."

Initially your future leaders will be found when you ask for help. It will come from within the team. Recognize when someone is stepping up to the plate and hold a desire to bring them up to your highest capability.

Bill Hybels wrote another book in 2004 (Zondervan, Grand Rapids, MI) titled, "The Volunteer Revolution, Unleashing the Power of Everybody. In Chapter 4, "The Great Exchange," he quotes Acts 20:35 – In everything I did, I showed you by this kind of hard work we must help the weak, remembering the words the Lord Jesus spoke, "It is more blesses to give than receive." But, it's at the end of chapter 5 where he tells us to "Lift the vision," "Accept the honor," and "Rise to the challenge."

Chapter 13

CONCLUSION

Then It Happened...

As I was praying for God's hand to touch this book, the final chapter was given to me. After reading this book and getting a glimpse into how your church's security could work, the message is filling in the blank to this opening statement – "Then it happened..." At the beginning of this book, I told you about Jeff R. Laster who was the first person to greet a stranger walking through the front door of his church. The visitor then opened fire killing eight and wounding seven others in an active shooter incident that happened at Wedgwood Baptist Church in Fort Worth, Texas, on September 19, 1999. Sitting in his hospital bed, Jeff asked himself, "What do you think you could have done differently?" Well, I hope I have provided some information that would have you answer that question now.

Then it happened...
We started implementing standard operating guidelines and began a regular monthly training for team members. Ushers, greeters, and others were invited to attend and learn our protocols. Visions and expectations

were unveiled, and we began sharing what we thought was fair for team members to expect from us.

We lost just a couple people who didn't see the value in the new changes, but that is typical of any organization. There were some rough patches with other team members and with a few employees. Recruiting efforts tripled our team size in just about a year and we are half way to our recruiting goal. Once the team became more recognizable, more people realized that we had a team they could join. Now, new people accept training as standard and are open to learning. Together, our team has put in the time and efforts to provide our church and its congregation with a better trained threat assessment and first response team capable of handling emergencies until outside agencies arrive.

It was not easy. There is no magic, only a lot of prayer and patience. Everyone did not buy into the transition immediately, some still don't, there were misunderstandings, and a couple team members did leave the ministry. But in the end…it was worth it and I don't believe anyone on our team would hesitate to go through the transition all over again. There is satisfaction in sacrifice and praise in excellence.

The team was tested on a hot Sunday in July. It was about a half hour before our second service, which is also the most attended service of the week, with about 2,500 congregants attending. An usher had just returned to church after a few weeks away for a hip surgery. He pulled me aside and showed me something he was concerned about, regarding a middle aged person who was kicked off the property a year earlier. I had met him and his family at our last Christmas production. The incident tore my heart out and it was the reason I began keeping a journal of what security was doing. In my opinion, the situation was not handled well.

The person in question is a white male, mid-thirties, unemployed, and homeless, with a meth addiction. His mother posts on Facebook that he has a condition called methamphetamine psychosis, as a result of his addiction. His children were taken away from him. And, about a day earlier, he was posting on his Facebook page that, "Christians were going to pay," which is a summary of many of his posts.

Here is one of his posts from Facebook: "Please… Brother and sister in

Christ.... stand with me. It might get you killed but hey... Matt 25:41-45 I love you guys. Pray for me tonight please."

There are other posts that are rants, but one underlying theme seems to be his judgment that certain people who won't help him are controlled by Satan and he will get his judgment.

People were funneling into the sanctuary. It was busy and the threatening posts didn't register with me right away. The team was in their positions, radios on, and the worship music started to play. That's when I was approached by a police officer who had been assigned to our church for quite a while and was aware of the situation.

He had no clue the usher showed me a Facebook page or that the person of interest's name had even come up, so it was quite concerning when the officer mentioned that the person of interest (POI) was seen in the building. Further, he said he was a bit miffed by the entire encounter as the officer's attention had been diverted away from the crowd in the hallway and this person made a concerted effort to walk up to him, tap him on the shoulder, and say good morning – something that just wasn't natural for anyone.

As we've described before, and I hope this gets through now, even the seasoned police officer took five seconds or more to register the face, evaluate the treat, and decide to follow him. But by that time the POI had blended in with hundreds of others and was in the sanctuary...somewhere.

The officer said he was carrying a shoulder bag and that it looked heavy. I radioed my team to let them know we were looking for this POI. Everyone was alert and looking trying to detect, waiting for the worst.

Tick, toc, tick, toc...time felt like it slowed down. Eventually, services were ending and the pastor prepared the congregants for an altar call - the audience stood up and engaged in prayer. Following team protocols, everyone in front kept their positions and backup was provided to protect the senior pastor. I made my way to the front of the stage and had to cross over a row, from one aisle to another. As I got there, I saw a perimeter of security, virtually unnoticed to the average church goer or the pastor, who I would imagine never knew anything was even wrong - until he reads about it in this book.

I can't tell you if the POI was deterred, but we never did find him. All the glory to God, but the team was prepared and fairly trained, which gave them confidence and satisfaction in their service. This story could have a worse ending – it's always possible, but this was a, "Then it happened…," moment – and so I can write, "Then it happened, and we were prepared," unlike people who will write about incidents and ponder what they could have done better.

Again, the answer is found in being prepared. Hopefully, I and other contributors I've cited have provided some insight into church risk assessments, security team purpose, goals, scope, and operational guidelines. We've covered recruiting, background checks, training, meetings, communications, and record keeping as well as the principles of Deter, Detect, Delay, and Deny and we discussed use of force and firearms. Information for best practices and training never stop.

Politics in the church is nothing new. It's something that is found in every organization - period. I've included some discussion on this, but in the end, the greatest advancements will be made by churches whose pastors and directors support the change to include a Volunteer Security/EMS Team.

We also talked about the importance of following insurance company coverage requirements and federal, state, and local laws. Know them and abide.

Other issues we didn't cover in this book include CPR and first aid training, how to operate an automated external defibrillator (AED), and church medical kits that now include gunshot treatments and a larger ability to respond to trauma. Basic drug store first aid kits, the kind you find in your home or car are no longer sufficient.

Any discussion of safety and risk management must include computer network and document security. There is a treasure trove of information kept on church computers. Computer hacking, even from a kid who is just doing it for a hobby, can negatively affect church records, accounts, personal information, and much more. An entire industry has been built on e-security.

We didn't talk much about physical security: camera systems, lighting, purposeful obstructions, building layout, locks, and a slew of other security concerns. And we didn't touch much on protecting kids on campus and off campus events. But, these concerns are also a very real part of protecting the flock.

The question of why security is needed is past answering. Chances are, you already have people in the role of security at your church, whether you formally acknowledge them or not. Regardless of how you view your security, unless you have assessed your risks and developed a security team that your church can control, you may one day face the tragedy that is affecting more and more places of worship all the time.

Please feel free to use these SOGs as a guide in setting up your team. May God keep you and your congregation safe, and may your team be a blessing to you and your church.

Appendix A

SOG TEMPLATE

Volunteer Security/EMS Team (VST) Standard Operating Guidelines (SOGs)

Purpose

(Your church name) Volunteer Security/EMS Team's (VST) purpose is to protect church employees, members, visitors, and property during church services, special events, and as requested, by serving as a real time threat assessment team and by providing pre-planned/coordinated first response until outside agencies arrive. VST's focus is providing safety, security, and emergency medical help during church services inside church structures, and as requested.

Matthew 10:16 – "Behold, I send you out as sheep amongst wolves; therefore be as wise as serpents and harmless as doves."

How this verse applies to church security goals and objectives is "wise as serpents" instructs us to "prepare in advance" and "harmless as doves" instructs us to "do so in a Christ-like way that compliments (Your church name) Church's **CORE MISSION** " … to lead people into a fully-devoted relationship with Jesus Christ by loving people, cultivating community, and inspiring hope."

(Your church name) Church's VST program objectives are to use Deter, Detect, Delay, and Deny as the model through which we will achieve our goals. The VST will respond to and recover from related events and assist with basic emergency medical services. We achieve this through creation of SOGs, proper vetting of volunteer safety personnel, training, and building relationships with local emergency providers, other worship safety/security teams, and the community. The VST, under the direction of church leadership, is committed to this program to positively impact the mission of our church.

Our mission is to help assure (Your church name) Church is a safe place where those who are seeking can find salvation through our Lord and Savior Jesus Christ.

SCOPE

The scope of the VST is limited to the activities inside the (Your church name) Church for a short period of time prior to worship services, during worship services, time between services, for a short period of time after services and includes special events like speakers and productions held on the (Your church name)Church premises as requested. VST may also provide services outside of buildings, including off campus events as requested. EMS team members are not required to perform security functions, but may do so, if they choose.

Goals

Team goals are as follows: Recruit, train, and operate a security/EMS team that will focus on the safety and security of the church before, during, and after worship services on church grounds or as requested for other church functions, and offer certified response for medical emergencies.

Inside our team, our goals are to offer fraternity to members and to rely on each other in our walk with Christ Jesus. We seek to build leaders and give purpose to those who sacrifice their time to serve by seeking excellence in mission and vision.

Team members will be assigned to specific pastors and will accept position assignments to assure their safety. Risks and responses will be detailed in training.

VST's primary focus is the safety of pastors and will always be our top consideration. As more safety team members arrive, the scope and perimeter of coverage may expand to include: people attending worship, children, church property and assets, protection against liability, and EMS response.

Appendix A: SOG Template | 189

As church campuses are added to the (Your church name) family, duplication of these SOGs and training to other campuses should be easy. The goal would be to have all churches on the same page with the VST and to establish clear communications and predictable response.

Standard Operating Guidelines
1.1 Membership

1. Any church member, who has been at (Your church name) Church for at least six (6) months, may apply to the VST for membership. We seek people who have the most important ingredients of all, those being: a shepherd's heart, integrity, commitment to a task and people skills. Any member with less than six months at the church must receive the approval of VST leaders.

    EMS volunteers must be a currently licensed CNA, EMT, Paramedic, Nurse, or Physician.

2. All potential VST members must complete the (your church name) Church application and complete a background check. Background checks to include criminal checks in all 50 states, employment and reference checks. These checks will be completed on all team members at least every two years or as requested. Team members who are absent for three (3) months or more will be required to submit to and pass a new background check.

3. After successfully passing the background check, the applicant will be interviewed by a church leader and/or security team member designated by the VST Director.

4. Volunteers must be able to attend (8) eight of (11) eleven scheduled training sessions, including (1) one mandatory full day training (1) one time annually and meet other commitments. If a volunteer will be driving vehicles owned by (Your church name) Church or any of its affiliates, a Motor Vehicle Check should be obtained. Church leadership may determine acceptable number of accidents, violations, and types that are acceptable.

EMS volunteers must provide a copy of their current certifications, are responsible for maintaining their certifications, and must provide copies of certifications at least annually. Any EMS volunteer that loses certification or is past their renewal deadline must notify the VST EMS leader. Only volunteers with current certification may participate as a VST member.

5. Removal from the VST will occur to any member found providing false information on their application or background check, or who willfully hides pertinent information. Misconduct, abuse of power, failure to follow the mission of the team (Your church name) Church or fulfilling responsibilities, and/or the inability to work as VST member are reasons for removal.

Any team member who does not participate or communicate their reason for absence longer than (3) three consecutive months will be removed from the team roster. Any team member who is dropped or removed from the list may reapply and must complete a new background check.

2.1 Training
Basic training on topics deemed important by the VST will be conducted and attendance documented. A training file for each member will be started and updated as new training is conducted. Training is the most important part of our VST program. On-going training will serve to increase interest and protect our church from changing threats and legal issues that often arise when no training or inadequate training occurs.

1. Training will occur one (1) time per month on the second Saturday of each month or as per VST Director.

2. One day per year will be dedicated to a mandatory all-day training.

3. Additional training sessions may be called by team leaders and/or may require time changes to accommodate outside instructors and guest speakers.

4. Training may include lecture style, class participation, practice drills, reading, internet research, and other methods of instruction.

Appendix A: SOG Template | 191

5. All team members will be notified in advance of meeting dates and location.

6. Safety team members are expected to make at least (8) eight of (11) eleven training sessions annually.

7. EMS team members must attend mandatory VST training, but are exempt from 2.1 (6) training requirements. EMS leader will determine any training for EMS volunteers.

VST Protocol:

1. VST members are expected to arrive at least twenty (30) minutes prior to the service they are volunteering for and stay at least 20 minutes after services have completed.
2. Notify team leader when late arrival or early leave is necessary.
3. Dress code: Unless otherwise indicated, VST members must wear the specified team attire/identification.
    a. No torn, stained, or unkempt clothing is allowed.
4. Sign in attendance book for each service.
5. Team members will know their assignments.
    a. Assignments may be changed at any time by team leadership.
    b. Assignments may be changed for special events.
6. Check out a radio and an ear piece.
    a. Radios need to be worn and "on" throughout VST member's time of service.
    b. Radios are to remain on campus, unless requested for an off campus event.
7. Team Leader will designate assignments.
    a. Report to assigned post.
    b. Leadership may reassign different areas before, during, and after services.
8. Five (5) minutes prior to service start team leaders will call for a position check.
    a. Position check order: see 4.1 Assignments.

9. Report any incidents and complete required documentation.

10. Turn in radio and ear piece at the end of shift. Report any broken or missing equipment.

11. Sign out.

3.2 VST EMS Protocol

1. Arrive 30 minutes prior to event start.
2. Stay at least 20 minutes after event end.
3. Check equipment in first-aid bag.
4. Check AED battery.
5. Respond to any requests from anywhere on campus.
6. Assure all paperwork is completed for any incidents.
7. Restock first-aid bag.

3.3.0 Communications Policy: (For Radio Communications – see Communication 6.0)
3.3.1 Personal
Sharing VST information with any person not on the VST is prohibited as personal information that is shared can be a liability for both the church and the team member.

3.3.2 Talking to Media/Cameras/Posting
Talking to any media at any time regarding anything related to (Your church name) Church, any of its pastors, staff, volunteers, campuses, operations, etc., by any team member is strictly prohibited. The only people authorized to talk with media on any subject regarding (Your church name) Church, any of its affiliates, any staff or volunteer, including the VST is someone specifically appointed by (Your church name) Church.

3.3.3 Social Media
Team members are also restricted from communicating or commenting on incidents on social media and are forbidden from posting, sharing, or replying to any posted verbiage, photographs or videos, including "like" or similar buttons.

4.1. Assignments
Assigned positions for all services and performances are as follows:

Someone will always be designated to shadow the Senior Pastor – this is a priority position. This is a "Personal Protection" position. The VST member performing this task may also accept a position assignment.

All other VST members will be assigned as follows:

1. 1st position: Aisle 1, front row.
2. 2nd position: Aisle 2, front row or close.
3. 3rd position: Aisle 3, front row or close.
4. 4th position: Aisle 4, front.
    a. Positions 1-4 are stationary, and do not provide backup
5. 5th position: Aisle 3 rear.
6. 6th position: Aisle 2 rear.
7. 7th position: Roamer – Covers all areas of church sanctuary.
8. 8th position: Roamer – Covers all areas of church sanctuary.
    a. Positions 5-8 provide backup to any area
9. 9th position: EMS – Locate anywhere, responds to medical calls only

4.2 Pre & Post service door assignments
1. Door 1 – Main door west entrance.

2. Door 2 – Main door lower north entrance.

3. Door 3 – Upper mezzanine.

4. Door 4 - Upper mezzanine.

5. Roamer - Covers doors 1, 2, 3, and 4 of main church, mezzanine 1 and 2, all stairways, public and nonpublic areas, parking lots, child check in, administration building, other classes and buildings.

5.1 Chain of Command
1. (Your Church name) Lead Executive Director oversees all campuses and the VST.

2. VST Director (TD) oversees all activities of the VST and will serve as Incident Commander until turned over to an outside agency.

3. EMS Director oversees all activities of the VST/EMS, including record maintenance for certifications and/or licenses of EMS members, assigns EMS members to regular events and as requested, communicates supply needs, and maintains equipment. EMS Director is Incident for all EMS calls, until relinquished to an outside agency.

4. VST and EMS Team Leader (TL) is assigned to lead the VST/EMS at a specific service or event and is responsible for prioritizing team member assignments and assures all team goals are met. VST TL assumes command when Directors are not present.

5. VST Assistant Team Leader (ATL) will help TL and will assume command when TD and TL are not present. ATL will fill function as TL when designated TL is not present.

6. VST/EMS Member: is a member of the church congregation in good standing, Greets worshippers warmly, always on the alert for people of interest, disrupters, intruders, vandals, etc. Follows the SOGs of deter, delay, detect, deny, respond to and

recover from loss events, and assist calling emergency medical services when needed. Communicates all facts to team members. Follows orders of Team Leader and may be designated as Team Leader when requested.

7. EMS members: Will respond to medical incidents, assess and provide proper treatment commensurate with their level of certification/licensing. Document incident on the proper form, and assist the security team where capable.

8. Should TD, TL, and ATL not be available, the following order will determine TL and if necessary, incident command: P11, P10, P9, P6, P5, P8, P7, P4, P3, P2, P1.

9. EMS – EMS is leader at all EMS responses.

6.0 Communications
Proper communications fulfills our goals of detection and response.

6.1.0 Proper Etiquette for Radio Use
1. Always use an earpiece properly attached to your radio to prevent speakers from being heard.

2. Earpieces may be provided by the church or purchased by VST member.

3. Use of profanity, inappropriate remarks, and outbursts of music is prohibited.

4. Identify yourself by your position, followed by the person you are trying to contact.

6.2.0. Radio Use
1. Radio Use:
   a. Use designated radio channel
      i. VST is channel 1.
      ii. Outside security is channel 2.
      iii. Special events – see posted channel being used by radio chargers.
   b. Know what you want to say before you key the mic.
   c. Make certain you are on the correct channel.

d. Wait a couple of seconds after keying the mic before speaking.
e. Keep it short and simple.
f. Remain calm, speak clearly.
g. Do not whisper. If necessary, use your hand to shield your voice.
h. Clear text – plain English should be used for all communications.
i. Remember – others are listening.

2. In an emergency
    a. State your position.
    b. State 9-1-1.

3. Report any radio or transmission problems to your team leader.

4. Radio communications are for VST essentials and response during services.

5. Radio check upon starting a shift.
    a. Announce check.
    b. Await response and acknowledge.
    c. If no response:
        i. Check that radio is turned on and on the correct channel.
        ii. If radio is on and channel correct, try a new headset.
        iii. If the problem was the headset, take the old headset and set it aside – let your team leader know it didn't work.
    d. If your radio was on and the headset is not the problem – get a different radio, put the old one aside, and inform the team leader.

6. Pre-service/event communications
    a. Discussing guest arrival, special needs, construction, detours, etc.
    b. Obtain clarification(s) from team leader.
    c. Relay pertinent information regarding "People of interest" (POI) or "Doesn't look right" (DLR).

7. Assignment confirmation:
   a. Five (5) minutes prior to services team members should be at their assigned posts.
   b. Team leader will request confirmation.
   c. Reply with your name and position assignment.

8. Reporting EMS incident by radio:
   a. Report location, person or people involved, a quick description, and if EMS is needed.
   b. Once on scene, EMS will decide if transport is necessary.
   c. EMS may call for additional supplies or assistance. Roamers and positions 5 and 6 will respond first.

9. Reporting Incidents:
   a. Report position assignment, where you are going, and why.
   b. Request backup or backup positions.
   c. Relay all known information:
      i. Person(s): gender, height, race, weight, age, clothing, distinguishing features. Vehicle(s): type, manufacturer, color, year, distinguishing features.
      ii. Location: signs of vandalism, break-in, safety concern, any special needs like clean up, person pick up, etc.
      iii. Other: Fire, loose animal, lost child, incoherent adult, suspected bomb, etc. Reporting a Person of Interest (POI) or something that doesn't look right (DLR):

10. DLR Person(s). Report:
    a. Gender, height, race, weight, age, clothing, distinguishing features.
    b. Detail why you feel this is someone to watch.
    c. Security leadership may determine that the POI should be denied entry. This call would require backup and an incident report. Obtain as much information as possible.
    d. If not detained, try and find where they are sitting.

e. If possible, take a picture of the DLR.
   i. Pictures you take, using your personal device, falls under the Social Media policy 3.3.0.

11. Non Person Report:
    a. Describe what you see and exactly where you are.
    b. Detail why this is important.
    c. Relay emergency response if needed.

12. Reporting any suspicious activity and safety concerns:
    a. People in areas where there should be no activity.
    b. Disruptions.
    c. Vandalism.
    d. Safety concerns.
    e. Emergencies.

6.2.0 Procedure for calling outside agencies.
1. Radio campus police officer or security guard and make your request for outside services.

2. If there is no campus coverage or no immediate answer use your cell phone and dial 9-1-1.
    a. Provide 9-1-1 dispatch with the following:
       i. Location information - Building number and physical reference
       ii. Church address: (List your church address).

3. Stay on the phone until 9-1-1 releases you.

4. Advise VST team on channel one (1) that an outside agency is responding to your call. VST team leader will advise outside security on channel 2.

5. Outside security will direct responding outside agencies. In their absence, a VST member may be asked to take on this responsibility.

7.0 VST Security Actions:
7.1 Deter
a. Allow your presence to be recognized.

Appendix A: SOG Template | 199

    b. Wear your VST identification.
    c. Greet attendees with a smile, warm welcome, and handshake.
    d. Assure your radio is operational and on.
    e. Assure your ear bud is in good working condition.
    f. Report to your assigned position and maintain it.
    g. Be ready to support another team member in your support zone.
    h. Communicate suspicious activity and Persons of Interest (POI).
    i. Crowd control is always important; do not allow situations to escalate via the crowd.

7.2 Detect
Dealing with disruptive behavior, such as shouting, cursing or trying to take control of services, must be dealt with quickly and with as little disruption of the service as possible.
    a. Be aware. Observe. Always pray with your head up and eyes open.
    b. Exercise heightened awareness always. Look for people/events that do not follow base patterns.
    c. Respond to church pastors, staff, volunteers and congregants.
    d. Communication - Alert the team.
    e. (Your church name) Church will notify VST Team leader of any received electronic, telephonic, written, or verbal threats:
        i. Threats
        ii. Staff
        iii. Volunteers
        iv. People attending worship
        v. Property
        vi. Suspicions reports, suspected potential threats
        vii. Angry spouse, significant other
        viii. Parent custody battle
        ix. Restraining orders
        x. Information from other ministries, parking lot, etc.

7.3 Delay
Delay strategies are to slow/disrupt perpetrator's attempts to access property and/or specific areas. Physical barriers may be applied, but it is important not to hinder access for emergency responders or routes for evacuation. Security team members may pose as a barrier with back up and team leader approval.

a. Attempt to verbally de-escalate the situation.
      i. Use verbal judo.
      ii. Tag out: After 30 seconds, if no success, allow backup to try verbal de-escalation.
   b. If unable to immediately de-escalate, instruct the person to go into the hallway for further discussion.
   c. Call for police backup.
   d. Effective delay tactics allow enough time-between detection and access-for law enforcement officials to respond and catch the intrusion in progress.
   e. Concentrate delay efforts away from likely targets in order to keep the intruder from accessing them before help arrives.
   f. Ask last question: "Is there anything I can say or do right now that will get you to cooperate with us?"
   g. "No" answer – go to Deny.

7.4 Deny
   a. The process of denial may be achieved through
      i. Barriers
      ii. Presence
      iii. Lock down
      iv. Physical denial as a last resort
   b. Communicate
   c. Call Police.
   d. Back up team members.
   e. Perimeter Response – direct incoming government agencies.
   f. Deploy VST identification.
   g. Assist calling emergency services.
   h. Obey all commands of incoming government agencies.

7.5.0 EMS Medical Incident – Procedures
Any VST member responding to an EMS call must always wear gloves where blood or bodily fluids are present. VST EMS only offers basic EMS first response, packaging and stabilization.
   a. Radio for help or designate someone else use the radio and call.
   b. Do not leave the patient alone to get help or supplies.
   c. Stay with the patient until the incident is over.

Decision Matrix
1. Can the patient be moved away from the public?
    a. If they have fallen, are complaining of head, neck, back, pelvic, or hip pain do not attempt to move them, except for cardiac arrest, to move them out of the sanctuary before treating if possible.
    b. For all other situations, if the person is ambulatory and they can walk on their own, move them away from the public.
    c. Do not "walk" any person that appears to be in distress. Call for a wheelchair or other walking assistance device.

Types of Medical incidents and their treatment
  a. Falls:
       i. If head neck, back, hip, or pelvic pain – consider calling fire department and DO NOT MOVE the patient.
       ii. Cuts and abrasions: Take appropriate actions to stop bleeding, clean and bandage.
       iii. Fractures, broken bones, sprains, and strains – splint or immobilize if possible, apply ice pack, consider calling fire department if unable to splint or needs ambulance for transport.

  b. Diabetics:
       i. Check blood sugar.
       ii. If reading is below 60 or unable to check blood sugar and patient verbalizes they "feel low," give juice and/or food if they are awake and alert enough to eat. If unresponsive, call fire department.

  c. Difficulty Breathing:
       i. Asthma: if mild difficulty breathing and patient thinks their inhaler will handle it, stay with patient and monitor results. If no relief or breathing becomes more difficult – call fire department.
       ii. All other cases – call fire department and give 15 liters oxygen by mask. Keep sitting upright. Do not lie down.

  d. Other Medical Problems: i.e. headaches, nausea, vomiting, do not feel well...

      i. Check blood pressure.
      ii. Consider calling fire department if needed or if patient requests it.

Incidents that require Fire Department MUST BE CALLED
a. Seizures
      i. Protect from injury
      ii. Apply oxygen by mask. Flow 15ml.
      iii. Very common for patients to wake confused and resistant. Do not force oxygen if resistant.

b. Weak or dizzy
      i. If systolic BP is under 100 – let them lie down and elevate legs if possible.
      ii. Check blood sugar. If below 60, give juice and/or food. Monitor progress.

c. Unconsciousness (fainting – usually 1 minute or less)
      i. If systolic BP 100 – let them lie down and elevate legs if possible.
      ii. Check blood sugar. If below 60, give juice and/or food. Monitor progress.

d. Chest pain
      i. Symptoms include tightness or heaviness in chest, pain radiates to arm, jaw, or neck. Suspect heart issues.
      ii. Keep patient sitting unless they feel like passing out or systolic BP is below 100. Then lie them down.
      iii. Apply oxygen by mask at high flow 15ml or 4ml with a nasal cannula.
      iv. Make sure systolic BP is above 120 before allowing a patient to take their own nitro pills.
      v. Keep patient calm and relaxed.

e. Abdominal pain
      i. Keep in position of comfort, either sitting or lying down.
      ii. Prepare for possible vomiting.

f. Strokes: Symptoms include the following: loss of feeling or movement on one side of the body, facial drooping, slurred speech, unable to speak or confused.
   i. Keep sitting upright if possible.
   ii. Apply oxygen by mask, flow 15ml or 4ml by nasal cannula.
   iii. Check blood sugar.

g. Cardiac arrest
   i. Use continuous chest compression CPR only.
   ii. Do not stop for any reason, until pulse returns.
   iii. Apply oxygen by mask, flow 15ml.
   iv. Have chest compressioners switch off every two (2) minutes for effective compressions.
   v. If trained medical personnel on scene, may bag valve mask respirations – after two (2) minutes of CPR have been completed.

Communications – see 6.2.0

7.6.0 VST Documentation
7.6.1 Security Documentation/Reporting
1. Minor issues that do not require documentation:
   a. POI/DLR alerts
   b. Normal requests from pastors, staff, volunteers, congregants, etc.
   c. Outside security issues where VST is not involved

2. Reports Requited
   a. All "Delay" events.
   b. All "Deny" events.
   c. Any time "Use of force" is applied.
   d. Anytime outside agencies are called in.
   e. Upon request.

3. Copies of all reports must be provided to the (Your church name) Church Security Director.

7.6.2 EMS Team Documentation/Reporting
Minor issues such as: handing out small bandages or performing blood

pressure checks does not require documentation. All other incidents require documentation.

1. Contact card for minor issues: cuts, abrasions, bumps, bruises, etc., where patient is ambulatory and either patient or legal guardian make decision not to seek additional treatment.

2. Contact Card Information Must Include:
    a. Patient Name.
    b. Name of parent or legal guardian if under 18.
    c. Date of Birth.
    d. Address.
    e. Phone number.
    f. Brief description of the problem and treatment.
    g. Name of EMS team member

3. Medical Incident Reports must be used for all other types of medical incidents. It will include all the information listed with the contact card and will include the following:
    a. Vital signs
    b. Recording times of treatments
    c. Recording time when fire department is called and when they arrive.
    d. An 8 ½ X 11 EMS report must be used

4. Copies of all reports must be provided to (Your church name) Church Director of Security

8.0 Use of Force
Typically, the flow of events, from the time it is recognized that additional help is necessary, should include alerting the on campus police officer and outside security of the need for their assistance. In their absence, VST members or a person they appoint may dial 911. The use of force policy is only applied when time prohibits alerting the on duty officer or (Paid church security if you have it) Security guards, the officer needs help, or a person/people are in immediate danger.

Team members will use physical force only to prevent injury to himself/

herself, or another person or, when necessary, and/or to remove a threat from church property.

1. Police must be called any time a person is restrained or force is used.

2. Only reasonable force necessary to subdue the threat may be used.

3. Security team members may initiate force at any time after de-escalation attempts have failed or at any time after a weapon has been identified or to defend against a physical attack on themselves, pastors, staff, volunteers, or congregants.
    a. You must document de-escalation attempts.
    b. You must provide a reason why you felt no other option was available.
    c. You must document exactly what the disrupter said and did.
    d. You must document the entire episode from beginning to end.

4. Use of force applies to:
    a. Physical threats
    b. Stopping actual physical violence
    c. Detaining a threat who has been positively identified in a criminal act
    d. Protecting others against actions that may endanger the health and safety of others nearby.

5. Restraining methods:
    a. May only be used when reasonable belief exists that a person presents an immediate threat.
    b. orce option or restraint may be used that prevents a person from speaking or breathing.
    c. Restraints may be removed after it is determined that the person no longer poses a threat or when they voluntarily leave the property.
    d. The only authorized restraints are contemporary name brand handcuffs.
    e. Leg-irons, ropes, straps, zip ties, or any other device, are not authorized for use.

6. Restraint techniques must be removed immediately:
   a. When at any time, a restrained person demonstrates signs of distress.
   b. EMS must be called.
   c. Every effort must be made to ensure the safety of anyone being restrained.

7. Justification – physical force
   a. VST members may use physical force if and to the extent that a reasonable person would believe it necessary to maintain order. A person acting under a reasonable belief that another person is about to commit suicide or to inflict serious physical injury upon himself may use physical force upon that person to the extent reasonably necessary to thwart the result.
   b. Reasonably believing a team member cannot safely withdraw from the encounter.
   c. Protecting a third person.
   d. Protecting against a crime in progress.

Justification – physical force
Security team members may use physical force if and to the extent that a reasonable person would believe it necessary to maintain order, but such person may use deadly physical force only if reasonably necessary to prevent death or serious physical injury.

1. A person acting under a reasonable belief that another person is about to commit suicide or to inflict serious physical injury upon himself may use physical force upon that person to the extent reasonably necessary to thwart the result.

2. Any other person, who renders emergency care at the scene of an emergency occurrence, may use reasonable physical force for the purpose of administering a recognized and lawful form of treatment and/or stabilization.

3. Reasonably believing a team member cannot safely withdraw from the encounter.

4. Protecting a third person.

5. Protecting against a crime in progress.

Justification – deadly force
A person is justified in threatening or using deadly physical force against a threat or disrupter:

1. If such person was threatening or using physical force against another.

2. To the degree a reasonable person would believe that deadly physical force is immediately necessary to protect himself against the other's use or attempted use of unlawful deadly physical force.

3. Team members have no duty to retreat before threatening or using deadly physical force.

4. Defense of a third person.

5. Protecting against a crime in progress, where deadly physical force is necessary to stop a crime in progress, such as arson, 1st or 2nd degree burglary, kidnapping, manslaughter, second or first degree murder, sexual conduct with a minor, sexual assault, child molestation, armed robbery, or aggravated assault that threatens the lives of others.

Reporting
1. Immediately report use of force incidents to the Team Leader.

2. Make reasonable efforts to obtain as much information about the threat including:
   a. Name
   b. Address
   c. Contact information
   d. Try and get a photograph

3. Team members who decide to use physical force must document why they determined this action was necessary. Include

any statements, weapons, sudden moves, personal feelings, actual occurrences (including the statements and information of witnesses) that caused you to believe that physical force was needed.

4. Indicate any obvious injuries to all parties involved, including pains.

5. Get detailed information about police, fire, EMS, and other responders, including congregants who may have helped security team members.

8.1: Firearms

Any VST member may conceal carry while performing security ministry services to the church as long as they meet mandatory team membership, training, and equipment requirements.

Team membership (see 1.1 Team Membership for details): Any team member who desires to carry a firearm while acting as a member of this team must be a member in good standing and comply with all team member requirements.

Training (see 2.1 Training): Training requirements as per 2.1 must be met, and additional firearm training requirements must be completed.

1. Requirements to Carry
   a. Must submit some form of firearms safety training.
   b. Must comply with all applicable Arizona or state statutes.
   c. Must participate in, and pass all firearms qualification courses, annually.
      i. Shoot don't shoot training
      ii. Combat firearm training
      iii. Range training and target scoring

Any sworn, certified, peace officer in the State of Arizona or an active federal government law enforcement officer may be exempt from these requirements.

Appendix A: SOG Template | 209

2. Procedures
   a. Firearms must be concealed at all times.
   b. No team member will unnecessarily draw, display or carelessly handle a firearm.
   c. All team members will immediately comply with all police orders.
   d. No team member may fire any warning shots.
   e. No team member may draw their weapon as a threat or use it to try and de-escalate a situation.
   f. Discharging a firearm is only appropriate to stop a life threatening threat.
   g. Always treat your firearm as if it loaded and the safety is off
   h. Be sure of your target and what is beyond it
   i. Always keep your finger off the trigger until ready to fire

3. Equipment
   a. Approved firearms are handguns with the following calibers: .380, 9mm, .38, .357, .40, and .45. Rifles, all other calibers, and other firearms are prohibited.
   b. Ammunition may only be hollow point ammunition.
   c. Ball, armor piercing, and hand loaded ammunition is not allowed.
   d. All firearms must be secured in a concealed holster at all times. Carrying an unapproved weapon is grounds for immediate termination from the team.

4. Other weapons
   It will be acceptable for VST members to carry certain self-defense weapons such as:
   - Pepper spray or mace
   - Tactical pen
   - Extending baton
   - Stun gun or Taser
   - Tactical flashlight
   - Knife

5. Weapons not allowed
   - Nun chucks
   - Swords
   - Anything that cannot be concealed.

9.0 Evacuation & Lockdown Procedures
Evacuation is the orderly movement of people and crowds to a safe zone.

Lockdown means securing people and crowds in place.

1. Know your roll in an evacuation. Be familiar with evacuation procedures from every post.

2. Know pre-planned designated meeting areas.

3. Ushers to assist with special needs evacuations.

4. Only the (Your church name here) Church Security Director and/or a VST Team Leader can call for an evacuation or a lockdown.

5. Stay calm. Help the crowd stay calm. Communicate safe zone information.

6. Do not allow people to return once evacuated.

7. VST will be responsible for communications with pastors, band, whoever is onstage.

8. Evacuating large numbers of people is a process that takes time.

9. If possible, isolate apparent danger to prevent further injury.

10. Direct emergency service personnel.

11. Reunite parents and children once in designated safety zones.

9.1 Evacuation & Lockdown Procedures:
911 personnel, VST, or emergency coordinators may instruct that the congregation is to evacuate or to remain in place depending on the type of emergency. Evacuation procedures may vary depending on the nature

of the emergency. Buildings will be evacuated when an alarm sounds or upon notification by emergency personnel. Be prepared to do the following:

Evacuation is the orderly movement of people and crowds to a safe zone.
- See "Evacuation Chart in Appendix "D" for zone information and pre-planned designated meeting areas.
- See "Evacuation Routes" in Appendix "D" for evacuation routes.

Lockdown means securing people and crowds in place.
- See "Lockdown Procedures" in Appendix "D."

Know your role in an evacuation/lockdown. Be familiar with evacuation/lockdown procedures from every position.
- Ushers to assist with special needs evacuation.
- In prolonged lockdown situations, Ushers obtain medical needs information.

Only the (Your church name) Church Senior Pastor, Pastor in charge of Volunteer Security, VST Director, Security Director, anyone assigned as Executive Protection Team, or a Security Team Leader can call for an evacuation/lockdown.
- Activate the building's alarm if emergency personnel tell you to do so, or if it is apparent that people will be harmed if they do not leave (i.e. fire).
- Stay Calm.
- Help the crowd stay calm.
- In an evacuation, communicate evacuation routs and safe zone information.
- Instruct people that once outside, leave the immediate area, or go to a safe zone for further instructions.
- Do not allow people to return to the evacuated area until advised that it is safe to do so by emergency personnel.

Some emergencies may require that you take shelter inside buildings. Incidents such as a hostile person, severe weather or a hazardous material release are examples of times when you may be asked to stay in a specific area.

Public Safety & Security or law enforcement and emergency personnel will instruct you to evacuate or remain in place depending on the nature and context of the emergency. Do not sound any alarm in a lockdown situation.

If you are ordered to lock down an area:
- Go to the closest building.
- Close windows and doors and stay away from them.
- Lock doors if possible.
- Turn off air-conditioning, ventilation and lighting if possible.
- Close window coverings.
- Remain quiet and in place until notified by emergency personnel.
- Silence phones and do not use them unless you are calling emergency personnel
- In the main church, secure locking doors, stay away from windows in the stairways.
- Once doors are secure, they may not be opened without a police officer present.
- Have congregants fill out a "Get Connected Card," and list anyone who is missing from their group.

Set up Command Center
- Security office in main church. Any office in any other building.
- Provide Worship Security Team communications with outside agencies.
    - o Use channel 1, unless otherwise instructed.
- Copy of building blueprints kept in Worship Security office.

Appendix B

WORSHIP SECURITY INCIDENT REPORT

(Your Church Name) Volunteer Security Team Incident Report

Campus:_____ Date:_____ By:_____

Brief Description:

```
┌─────────────────────────────────────────────────┐
│                                                 │
│                                                 │
│                                                 │
│                                                 │
│                                                 │
│                                                 │
│                                                 │
│                                                 │
└─────────────────────────────────────────────────┘
```

Person Involved Name: _____ DOB_____

Address:_____Phone:_____

Witness Name:_____Phone:_____

Witness Name:_____Phone:_____

DCC Assigned Officer: _____

Outside Agencies: Police __   Fire __   EMS__   Other__

Incident Reference: _____

Additional Information Attached: _____

Appendix C

THREAT CHECKLIST

Threat Checklist
Complete this list if you receive a phone threat.

Exact time of call: _____ Date: _____

Exact words of caller:

_____

_____

_____

_____

Caller's voice: (circle) Male Female Adult Youth Estimate Age: _____

Black White Hispanic Asian Other: _____

Describe voice (circle all that apply): Calm Disguised Nasal Rapid Accent Nervous Angry Sincere Slurred Loud Excited Giggling Stressed Crying

If voice is familiar, whose did it sound like? _____

Background Noise: (circle) Music Children Typing Airplanes Machinery Cars/Trucks Other: _____

_____

Do not hang up! Obtain as much information as possible:

- When is the bomb going to explode? _____

- Where is the bomb? _____

- What does it look like? _____
- What kind of bomb is it? _____
- Method of activation: mechanical, clock, movement/chemical action? _____
- Method of deactivation? _____
- Did you place the bomb? _____
- Why? _____
- Where are you calling from? _____
- What is your address? _____
- What is your name? _____

Call received by: _____ Department: _____ Ext: _____

Note: In the event you receive a bomb threat:
- Call 911 immediately.
- Provide the following information:
    - Identify yourself
    - State: I have received a bomb threat.
    - Give your office location and extension.
- **REMAIN CALM!**

Appendix D

TRAINING OUTLINE

Volunteer Security Monthly Meeting/Training – Outline

Date: _____

Section 1: Worship Security Team Meeting (10-15 min)
a. Worship and prayer
b. Personal message from Team Leader
c. Roll call
d. Introduction of guests – non security team
e. Introduction of new team members
f. Announcements
g. Any follow up from previous meeting
h. Ask for mentor reports
i. Ask: Anything new we should be thinking about
j. Ask: Anything anyone wants to discuss since our last meeting
k. Questions for clarification

Section 2: Volunteer Security Team Classroom (10-20 min) – White Board & Markers
1. SOGs
    a. 1.1 - Membership
    b. 3.1 – Protocol
    c. 4.1 – Assignments/backup
    d. 5.1 – Chain of command
    e. 6.1 - Communications
    f. 7.1 - Actions
    g. 9.1 – Media communications

Section 3: Volunteer Security Team Practical (30-45 min)
a. 4.1 - Reactions
b. 6.1 - Communications
c. 7.1 - Actions

Meeting/Training Agenda filed with Roll Call Attendance

Appendix E

VOLUNTEER SECURITY TEAM

Accountability Sheet – option 1

Date: _____ Campus: _____

Security Positions Before/During Services

20 Minutes before services:

Position	Name
Door 1	
Door 1	
Door 2	
Door 3	
Door 4	
Sanctuary	
Sanctuary	

Positions during service:

Position	Name	Radio Number
1 – Stage Left		
2 – Center Stage Area		
3 – Stage Right		
4 – Aisle 3 Back		
5 – Aisle 2 Back		
6 – Roam		

7 - Roam		
8 – Back Stage		
9 - EMS		
10 -		

Volunteer Security Team Accountability Sheet – option 2

Campus: _____

Security Positions Before/During Services

Date_____ Service Time_____

Name	Radio Number

Appendix F

BLOODBORNE PATHOGENS

(Your Church Name) Church
All Campuses

Blood Borne Pathogens Information Sheet for Volunteers

This information is designed to assist you in knowing how to avoid and deal with possible exposure to a blood borne pathogen exposure. The American Red Cross offers several classes on this topic.

What are Blood Borne Pathogens (BBPs)? BBPs are communicable viruses that are passed from person to person through interpersonal contact with infectious blood or through other bodily fluids.

Most Prevalent Types:

HIV/AIDS
1. HIV is the name of the virus. A person with HIV may be symptom-free until it develops into AIDS.

2. The virus is very weak. It cannot survive long outside of the body or on environmental surfaces.

3. The virus cannot be transmitted by sweat, tears or insects.

4. An infected person's blood remains contagious and there is no cure.

HBV (Hepatitis B)
1. HBV affects the liver and its functions in the body.

2. Unlike HIV, this virus is very hardy and can survive on a surface up to 10 days.

3. About 1/3 of the carriers of HBV don't have symptoms and don't know they have it; 1/3 have mild flu-like symptoms; and 1/3 have severe symptoms and require hospitalization.

4. 10% of all people with HBV are chronic carriers of the disease and many do not even know they have it.

How do I protect myself?
1. Wear gloves before approaching a situation involving potentially infectious material: blood or any bodily fluids. Gloves are available in the Volunteer Security Team office. Carry a pair with you.

2. We don't train breathing for CPR, but if you are inclined to use breathing, use a mouth shield when performing CPR.

3. Practice good hand-washing and thorough drying procedures: after removing gloves, after using the bathroom and before handling any food.

4. Obtain the HBV vaccinations which can produce 97% effective antibodies and last for approximately 7 years.

5. Use a mechanical device (broom and dustpan or tongs) to pick up sharp objects (broken glass, etc.) rather than your hands. Wrap and/or tape sharp objects in cardboard for disposal.

6. Label bio-hazardous waste and dispose of materials correctly.

7. Use an approved virucide or 1/10 solution (1 part bleach to 10 parts water) in a labeled bottle. (See next section for cleaning up a potentially virulent spill.)

8. Practice good housekeeping and keep work areas clean.

9. Use Universal Precautions: Treat everyone as if they are carriers of the disease!

How do I clean up an accident? (Bloodborne Pathogen cleanup kits are available in the Volunteer Security Team office)
1. Put on gloves before approaching a scene with potentially infectious fluids.

2. Cover the contaminated area with paper towels.

3. Saturate with an approved sanitizer/virucide. (Or use a 1:10 solution – 1 part bleach to 10 parts water in a labeled bottle. Bleach solutions must be mixed only at the time of use.)

4. Wipe the area and dispose of the paper towels in the designated bio-hazard bag.

5. Repeat until material has been removed from area.

6. Respray area and allow to air dry for 10 minutes.

7. Wipe the area again.

8. Properly remove gloves to prevent contamination.

9. Properly dispose of materials. Label biohazardous waste and sharps or use the proper disposable materials (bright orange or red bags or containers marked with the black emblem.)

What do I do when/if I come in direct contact with blood or an infectious bodily fluid?
1. If you were wearing protective barriers and nothing touched exposed skin, it is not an exposure incident.

2. If contact was made, stabilize the situation, then immediately stop what you are doing and contact your physician to determine the need for potential exposure assessment.

3. If tested and the result is positive, an HBIG vaccination (85% effective in preventing the virus from manifesting) may be offered.

4. I have received a copy of the above information regarding blood borne pathogens to use as a reference in my volunteer position with the (Your Church Name) Volunteer Security Ministry.

Volunteer Name (print) _____ Date _____

Volunteer Signature _____ Date _____

Bibliography

Bill Hybels, the Volunteer Revolution, Unleashing the Power of Everybody, Zondervan, Grand Rapids, Michigan 2004.

Bill Hybels, Courageous Leadership, Field-Tested Strategy for the 360° Leader, Zondervan, Grand Rapids, Michigan, 2001 & 2009.

Brotherhood Mutual Insurance Company, The New Big Book of Checklists - Risk Management Checklists for Ministries, www.brotherhoodmutual.com

Carl Chinn, Evil Invades Sanctuary, The Case for Security in Faith Based Organizations, Snowfall Press, 2012

Curtis Hairston, Who Is Watching While They Pray, Canada, Hairston Handgun Firearms Training, 2013

David Grossman (Lt. Col.), Sheepdogs, Meet Our Nations Warriors, Delta Defense, Jackson WI, 2013

David Grossman (Lt. Col.) The Bulletproof Mind, Prevailing in Violent Encounters…and After, Dave Grossman & Gavin de Becker, 2006.
Daniel Blevens, The Armed Discussion in Your Church, CV Ministries, 2017

Dena Weiss, The Crime Scene: Tips For How First Responders Can Help Preserve Key Evidence, http:inpublicsafety.con, 2014

Fellowshipone.com, 7 Essentials for Church Security

FEMA - Department of Homeland Security, Guide for Developing High-Quality Emergency Operations Plans for Houses of Worship, USA, US Government, 2013

Gavin de Becker, Fear Less, Real Truth About Risk, Safety, and Security in a Time of Terrorism, United States of America, Little, Brown, and Company, 2002

Gavin de Becker, The Gift of Fear, Survival Signals That Protect Us From Violence, United States of America, Little, Brown, and Company, 1997

Gavin de Becker, Protecting the Gift, Keeping Children Safe (and Parents Sane), New York, New York, Dell Trade Paperback, 1999

George J. Thompson, PH.D., and Jerry B. Jenkins, Verbal Judo, The Gentle Art of Persuasion, William Morrow, Harper Collins Publishers, USA, 2013

Graham Kelly, Your Company's Purpose is not It's Vision, Harvard Business Review, HBR BLOG POST September 3, 2014

JD Hall, Protecting Your Church Against Mass Violence, pulpitandpen.org, 2015

John Baldoni, Lead with Purpose, Giving Your Organization a Reason to Believe in Itself, American Management Association, USA, 2012

Joseph A. Davis Ph. D, Critical Incident Stress Debriefing From a Traumatic Event, Posttraumatic Stress Following a Critical Incident, www.psychology today.com, 2013

Kevin Robertson, Church Security, Providing a Safe Worship Environment, Rancho Santa Margarita, CA, Pastors.com, 2014

Lisa Marie Dias, 7 Touches – a Basic Marketing Principle in Action, lisamariediasdesignes.com, 2013

Mennonite Mutual Insurance Company, Guns in Churches, Addressing Church Security Needs, www. mennonitemutual.com, 2013

Mike Shreve, 6 Earmarks of a Modern Day Esther, Charismagazine, 2015

Pablo Birriel, The Ministry Of Defense, Executive Protection For The Ministry, Hampton, Virginia, CFI Publishing, 2006

Patrick Van Horne and Jason A. Riley, Left of Bang, How The Marine Corps' Combat Hunter Program Can Save Your Life, New York, New York, Black Irish Entertainment LLC, 2014

Police Magazine, 5 Ways to Prevent Crime Against Churches, www.policemagazine.com, 2012

Robert M. Critin, Church Safety and Security, A Practical Guide, Lima, Ohio, CSS Publishing Company, 2005

Robert H. Welch, Serving By Safeguarding Your Church, Grand Rapids, Michigan, Zondervan, 2002

Ron Aguiar, Keeping Your Church Safe, United States, Xulon Press, 2008

Rory Miller, Facing Violence, Preparing for the Unexpected, Wolfboro, N.H.USA, YMAA Publication Center, 2011

Rory Miller and Lawrence A. Kane, Scaling Force, dynamic decision-making under threat of violence, Wolfeboro, NH, USA, YMAA Publication Center, Inc. 2012

Sara Horn, Safety in the Sanctuary: Is Your Church Prepared? www.preaching.com/resources/articles/11605335/ , 2009

Sun Tzu, The Art of War, 5th Century B.C

Tina Lewis Rowe, How to Assess the Safety and Security of your Place of Worship, http://tinalewisrowe.com, 2009

Resources

Book Resources
Federal

FEMA.gov
Infraguard.com
OSHA.gov

Businesses and Organiziations

Association of Threat Assessment Professionals, ATAP.com
ASIS International, ASIS.com
Christian Emergency Network (CEN) www.christianemergencynetwork.org
Charles W. Chadwick, JR. NOCSSM, NOCSSM.org
Gatekeeper Security, www.gatekeepersecurity.com
National Organization of Church Security and Safety Management, nocssm.org
Rock Church Safety and Security Conference, 2016

Other

Bible Study Verses, www.biblestudytools.com
Carl Chinn, www.carlchinn.com
Hartford Institute for Religion Research, hirr.harstem.edu
Legal-dictionary.thefreedictionary.com
Missouri Faith Based Homeland Security Initiative, dps.mo.gov/dir/programs/ohs/initiatives/
Wikipedia, www.wikipedia.org

Team Resources

Federal, State, Local

Department of Homeland Security (DHS):
Houses of Worship - Guide for Developing High-Quality Emergency Operations Plans for Houses of Worship.

www.dhs.gov/sites/default/files/publications/Developing_EOPs_for_Houses_of_Worship_FINAL.PDF

Active Shooter Workshop Participant
Whether you are able to attend a workshop or not, you may start developing an emergency action plan and access other informative materials.

https://www.dhs.gov/active-shooter-workshop-participant

If You See Something, Say Something® | Homeland Security
"If You See Something, Say Something®" engages the public in protecting our homeland through awareness–building, partnerships, and other outreach.
https://www.dhs.gov/see-something-say-something

Also available through DHS:

Conducting Security Assessments: A Guide for Schools and Houses of Worship Webinar, Business Continuity Planning Suite, and more.

Federal Bureau of Investigation (FBI):
InfraGuard program
InfraGard is a partnership between the FBI and members of the private

sector. The InfraGard program provides a vehicle for seamless public-private collaboration with government that expedites the timely exchange of information and promotes mutual learning opportunities relevant to the protection of Critical Infrastructure.

As an InfraGuard member, I have received many excellent training opportunities, updates, and resources. There is no cost to join. Applicants must pass an FBI background check.

https://www.infraguard.org/Application/General/NewApplication

Federal Emergency Management Agency (FEMA)
FEMA is an agency of the United States Department of Homeland Security. The agency's primary purpose is to coordinate the response to a disaster that has occurred in the United States and that overwhelms the resources of local and state authorities.

Emergency Management Institute (EMI)
EMI offers credentials and training opportunities for United States Citizens. Note that students do not have to be employed by FEMA or be a federal employee for some of the programs.
EMI maintains a strategic partnership with Frederick Community College (FCC). FCC has contracted with the Emergency Management Institute to provide college credit for the Independent Study Program (ISP). FCC offers eight specialized Letters of Recognition, an Undergraduate Certificate, and an Associate of Applied Science degree in Emergency Management.

Courses include: Emergency management, Safety and Security, and more.

https://www.firstrespondertraining.gov/frt/npccatalog/EMI

Independent Study Exams now require a FEMA Student Identification (SID) Number.

If you do not yet have a SID, register for one today: **https://cdp.dhs.gov/femasid**.

Introduction to Incident Command System, ICS-100; IS-700.a
https://training.fema.gov/is/crslist.aspx

Center for Faith-Based & Neighborhood Partnerships
https://www.fema.gov/faith

For more information on NIMS and ICS, please see **http://www.fema.gov/national-incident-management-system**.

FEMA Nonprofit Security Grant Program
The Nonprofit Security Grant Program plays an important role in the implementation of the National Preparedness System by supporting the development and sustainment of core capabilities. Core capabilities are essential for the execution of each of the five mission areas outlined in the National Preparedness Goal.
https://www.fema.gov/nonprofit-security-grant-program

State Fusion Centers:
Fusion centers operate as state and major urban area focal points for the receipt, analysis, gathering, and sharing of threat-related information between federal; state, local, tribal, territorial (SLTT); and private sector partners.

Community Liaison Program (CLP)
CLP is a conduit for assimilating information flow "To and From" law enforcement agencies into impacted communities. This results in the ability

to share information faster through a Redaction Process (compiling & building multiple sources of information into one single form) via DHS/FBI bulletins.

Church Risk Assessment
Through our CLP, DHS and our municipal police department performed a free risk assessment of our church.

State and Local
Also, feel free contact your State and Local Emergency Management to see if they have any resources for faith based houses of worship.

County and municipal law enforcement and fire departments usually have outreach programs and can be a great resource - use them.

Organiziations
ASIS International
Founded in 1955, ASIS International is the world's largest membership organization for security professionals. With hundreds of chapters across the globe, ASIS is recognized as the premier source for learning, board-certification, networking, standards, and research.
https://www.asisonline.org/

Christian Emergency Network (CEN)
CEN is a grassroots network equipping Christians to serve communities in crisis. The ReadyChristian, ReadyChurch and ReadyCity curriculum presents a preparedness and action plan for response.

Join Ready Christian & Ready Church

www.christianemergencynetwork.org

Faith Based Security Network (FBSN)

FBSN is a non-profit network that goes beyond individual preparedness to bring together the people of all types and locations of ministries as a national connected network.

The FBSN is a religious non-profit organization serving faith-based security and interested law-enforcement professionals with 5 services critical to improving American FBO readiness: Networking, Benchmarks, Best Practices & Resources, Threat intelligence sharing and models, and Public Policy and a representative legislative voice.

http://www.carlchinn.com/faith-based-security-network-inc..html

Coming soon:
Protect the Flock
A nonprofit organization dedicated to best practices for church security and addressing liability issues of volunteers

Protecttheflock.org
Security Training

Security training is a list of training that I have attended and found to be very good. This is by no means a full listing. As more and more churches start and improve volunteer security teams, the field of training opportunities will continue to grow.

National Organization of Church Security and Safety Management,

National Organization of Church Security & Safety Management

Resources | 235

(NOCSSM™) is a national organization of churches across the United States. We provide our members with educational resources to help them in their security efforts. Resources include our web site which includes written policy and procedure templates, best practices for church security and training videos from some of our national conference sessions of special interest to church security teams.

nocssm.org

San Diego Security Conference (Rock Church)
This conference will provide resources to help you fine-tune your safety and security plan. Whether your concern is your Children's Ministry, Youth Department, Risk Assessments/asset management, minimizing civil liability, or preparing the church for a safe worship service or large event, protecting your congregation and your facility is of paramount importance.
http://www.sdsecurityconference.com

Sheepdog Seminars
The Sheepdog Seminar is is a response to the violence that wreaks havoc in our world. It calls upon the defenders to take their stand.

In a one day seminar it is impossible to impart all of the information that churches - and society as a whole - need in order to create a safe atmosphere for their communities. However, when you leave the Sheepdog Seminar, you will know exactly what you need to start doing.

www.sheepdogsafetytraining.com

Strategos International
Strategos International, an innovative leader in security training, con-

sulting and protective services, is here to safeguard people and property. We can equip your organization to analyze, anticipate and overcome threats from without and within.

https://www.strategosintl.com

Campus Safety Magazine

Campus Safety is a news and information network for campus security specialists. CS focuses on topics and trends related to college and school safety, hospital security, emergency management, law enforcement and more to keep security professionals informed and aware of best practices.

This is a free subscription I highly recommend.

https://www.campussafetymagazine.com

Made in the USA
San Bernardino, CA
09 June 2019